JESUS LOVES ME

H. L. Roush, Sr.

JESUS LOVES ME

Library of Congress Cataloging in Publication Data

Roush, Herbert L., 1925-
  Jesus loves me.

  Reprint of ed. Published by Roush, Belpre, Ohio.
  1. God—Love. 2. God—Worship and love. 3. Love (Theology). I. Title.
  BT140.R58   1978   231'.6   78-1991
  ISBN 0-89293-049-7

Other books by H.L. Roush, Sr. include:

Henry and the Great Society ♦ Until the Daybreak
Sounds of the Heart ♦ Prayer and the Bible ♦ Father's Day - 1995
Victory ♦ When Do You Take Papa's Car Keys? ♦ Dearly Beloved
Jesus Me Ama (Spanish Edition of Jesus Loves Me)

For Information about other books and tapes, contact:

JESUS Loves Me Ministry

3587 Clover Lane ♦ New Castle, PA 16105
For Phone Numbers go to Web Site
Email: info@jesuslovesme.org
Web Site: www.jesuslovesme.org

COVER DESIGN AND ART WORK BY JON F. EELLS

DEDICATION

First, to my Father and His altogether lovely Son, my Lord and Saviour, Jesus Christ, Who graciously revealed to my needy heart the true nature of real love. May they be glorified.

Second, to those nameless ones whose names are written in heaven, through whom He touched me with the reality of His love, and without whose patient ministry I could not otherwise have known or written these precious truths. May their joy be full in seeing some fruit of their labors.

Last, to all those who have languished in a loveless prison, ever reaching out in hope of discovering a true and lasting love, only to be further disappointed and discouraged; who perhaps have stopped reaching, to sit in their loneliness, watching others as they search. As God sent Titus to comfort the depressed Apostle Paul, may He send this comfort to your lonely prison and free you to the light and liberty of His eternal love. May your heart-assured conviction be: "Jesus loves me, this I know." To these ones, and to these ends, I dedicate this book.

i

CONTENTS

PREFACE

This may well be the most important thing I have ever written, and perhaps the very last before our Lord Jesus Christ is revealed in all of His loveliness to those who now wait for Him. Should the Holy Spirit be pleased to anoint this message, it will help more people—unlock more prisons—free more slaves—answer more questions—and relate more truth to life as it really is, than any other effort I have ever made.

The discovery I have made about the nature of love has changed my life and re-directed the course of my ministry from that of mere theological mathematics, to the imparting of the personal love of Jesus to others. It has been a wing that has enabled me to better run the race of life for His glory. It has opened up new realms of love, fellowship and encouragement, and has been a precious gift of God in answer to my many years of reaching out for real love.

It is a message I *must* give. It embraces and explains the essence of all I have discovered and believe. The treasure of my heart is poured out on these pages with much prayer and many tears, that the reader will hear, in the secret place of his heart, this voice crying in the wilderness.

This is not a book addressed to the intellect. I have made no effort to develop a pleasing literary style. I make no apologies for what may appear to be repetition, crudeness, or over-simplification. My desire has been simply to talk heart to heart with you, the reader.

It is not a book written to the theologian. I have not been concerned with giving endless scripture references. My purpose is to tell the story of God's love as my heart has learned it. Anything I need to "prove" to you will only satisfy your mind. I trust that it will be with you as it was with Lydia—that the Lord Himself will open your *heart* to attend to the things I have spoken.

While I was talking with someone about the reality of love, they responded with, "Thanks for listening." I replied, "I did all the talking," and they answered, "But when you talk, you listen." May this book say all you have desired to say for so long, and may I have the precious privilege of listening to your heart, as you hear mine.

INTRODUCTION

"As he spake these words, many believed on him. Then said Jesus to those Jews which believed on him, If ye continue in my word, then are ye my disciples indeed; And ye shall know the truth, and the truth shall make you free. They answered him, We be Abraham's seed, and were never in bondage to any man: how sayest thou, Ye shall be made free? Jesus answered them, Verily, verily, I say unto you, Whosoever committeth sin is the servant of sin. And the servant abideth not in the house for ever: but the Son abideth ever. If the Son therefore shall make you free, ye shall be free indeed."

John 8:30-36

* * * * *

None of us likes to admit the possibility of being a slave. We boast about who we are, and are repulsed by the idea of anyone or anything infringing upon our freedom. But bondage is not always to man. It can also hold us in the prison of ideas, opinions and thought patterns. The bondage Jesus spoke about was a spiritual bondage; and the path to freedom was the truth.

Since the day I became a Christian, Jesus has sought to free me from the bondage of the mind. He does this by constantly bringing me to life situations whose pressing circumstances test the validity of my ideas and understanding. Since it is common to all the saints to love Jesus (and He is the Truth), it is natural that when our circumstances and experiences bend our ideas and opinions out of shape, we are driven to Jesus for truth with the suspicion that we have been in bondage to lies and deception.

I think of myself often as a scientist or mathematician, with my spiritual ideas, convictions and values all neatly formulated and filed in order. These calculations have been formed over the years; and as long as they work, I need never seek other answers nor question their correctness. Then one day, some life situation develops to which I apply what I believe to be the truth, and find that the "truth" doesn't fit the facts of the case, nor meet the needs of the heart. In other words, two plus two no longer equals four, but begins to equal five instead. Over and over I go again, adding the factors in the light I believe I have, and still the answer is wrong.

I know the truth of God cannot lie, so somehow my situation or circumstance will have to bend around the fixed truth of God, as space bends around matter. But when neither the circumstance nor the truth will bend, then I must suspect some miscalculation. Turning to the Word of God, I search to discover if the "truth" I have applied is *really* truth, or if I am like the Pharisees of old who held on to mere traditions of men, while believing them to be the commandments of God.

I desire, with the grace of God enabling me,

never to become a preacher of mere theology. I have always been revolted by men who are simply dispensers of religious theory. The doctrines we preach must work in life as well as in theory. They must stand unscratched by the abrasives of life; untarnished by the constant contact with reality; and cured in the furnace of friction and fact of experience. There seems to be too much preaching of neat theories that state spiritual equations and demand right answers based on them. But neither the loudness of the voice, nor the sincerity and genuineness of the appeal, will ever quiet the choked voice within that cries out against the unreality of these equations in actual life experience.

It is not that men are deliberate hypocrites, for no man enjoys the bondage of wearing a mask. But Satan is the master deceiver; and no deception is quite as sinister as the deception that we are not deceived when in reality, we are—that we are not in bondage to any, when in fact, we are. If the "light" we imagine ourselves to have within is really darkness, how great is that darkness!

So I have always feared falling into the lethargy of merely repeating pulpit phrases, no matter how pious they sound—doctrinal dogmas—theological concepts—intellectual utterances that impress those that listen, while knowing in my heart of hearts that the pompous propoundments I give out do not meet the needs of the heart in the reality of life's experiences.

As far as I am concerned, the only true doctrine is that which *works*. The only real truth is that which liberates us and frees us from whatever it promises to free us. That is, in my thinking, the real proof of the gospel of grace. It promises, and makes good on its promises. Paul meant to tell us this when he said,

> *"For I am not ashamed of the gospel of Christ: for it is the power of God unto salvation to every one that believeth; to the Jew first, and also to the Greek."*

He never feared that the gospel he preached would fail to work in any man who believed it, whether he be Jew or Gentile. He never feared that the gospel put to the test of reality in any man's life, would fail to meet the needs of his heart. No man would ever be ashamed, or put to the blush, after calling upon the name of the Lord in real faith.

The world around us is dying for real love. Not the false, shallow, meaningless love the songwriters describe and poets write about, but love that will stand the test of life, and endure. Men everywhere are crying out in their loneliness for love that will meet the needs of their hearts, answer their questions, solve life's love problems, and give some reason to the unreasonableness of their existence. We who profess the truth must be sure we do not mock them with empty equations and meaningless mathematics that do not match the facts of life. We cannot proclaim that we have peace when we have none. Our message must be one that is lived; and so the preaching must come from a rested and satisfied heart.

When our equations work only on paper, then we are deceivers if we insist that others labor in the same frustration. Much better to return to the Word of God with the broken pieces of our lives, and submit them to the truth to be fitted together in some meaningful pattern. Perhaps we have had some faulty understanding, some partial revelation, some half-truth that has kept us in shadows; or some concept, received by tradition, that we have accepted without question as to its truthfulness.

The only requirement to knowing the truth as it is in Christ, is the willingness to receive it. If we sincerely love and desire the truth, even at the risk of having our high and mighty minds changed about our position, we shall receive all we seek. Jesus promised,

"If any man will do his will, he shall know of the doctrine, whether it be of God . . . ."

The sincere heart that reaches out to Jesus will never be denied; and when he knocks, it shall be opened to him. When the honest lover of truth seeks, he shall find; and those who thirst and come to Jesus, shall abundantly be satisfied.

The precious truth I seek to write in this book was learned by the above method. The way of truth is solitary, and those who set out on it are lonely. Hence, the spiritual research I speak about was carried on in the mystery and loneliness of the laboratory of the heart, where none could see and understand but Jesus. As is true of all research, it has cost much, but not nearly as much as it cost

1) Doctrine must coincide w/ reality of life
2) Man are dying for love ←
3) Christians have an answer? that fits reality?

God to demonstrate the sincerity and reality of His love for me. I trust the benefits you receive as you read this book will be as satisfying as those I have received in learning and writing these precious things.

After Pilate had written the superscription to be placed over Jesus' cross, the Jews insisted that he change the wording from *"Jesus of Na-:areth the King of the Jews"* to *"He* said, *I am King of the Jews."* With much wisdom <u>Pilate</u> answered, *"What I have written I have written."* Somehow he knew that he had written the truth of God, though his reason could not fully comprehend it. <u>Daniel</u> wrote his prophecy by the revelation of God and sealed the book without fully understanding what he had written. <u>Paul</u> learned things he was never able to utter, for there were not enough words to convey the grandeur of what he had seen. So <u>I must confess that though there be much in this book that I do</u> not fully comprehend, my heart bears witness to the truthfulness of it. But, after all, if we waited to hear the truth of God from a mortal who fully understood and in whose life it had all been perfected, we would wait forever. Let us remember that the heart has its reason, that reason cannot understand.

It is not my intention to pass any judgments nor to build any fortress of dogma to which all must flee for safety or perish. I seek merely to explain what I have discovered; and explanations are only for the purpose of helping us understand what perhaps we have already learned in our hearts.

x

LOVE SEEKS YOU

I seek Love.

One of the most common cries of the human heart is: "No one understands me." All of us, at one time or another, have expressed the frustration of the inner man with these solemn words. It is not merely a statement of self-pity, as we are often told, but the honest realization that we live lives of quiet desperation. We sense that there is so much more to us than others comprehend, and we yearn for someone to reach and hear us. We see ourselves like actors playing our appointed roles in society and the home, projecting the image our part demands, while the real person we know ourselves to be remains unknown. The example of the clown who weeps behind his mask is familiar to all of us. The desire to "be ourselves" overwhelms us often, but just as often is stifled in the realization that only further misunderstanding and rejection will follow.

This concept of our personalities is not new to modern man. Those who peopled Japan in ancient times had this concept of the soul: "the little man inside." The pygmies of Africa, almost the lowest in the human scale, have a word in their language for soul that means "man on the inside." We often glimpse this undeniable fact and see ourselves imprisoned and isolated while surrounded by those who claim to know and love us. Many have reconciled themselves to a lifetime of loneliness after reaching out without success to others.

1

Exiled and alone, they sit in silence watching others while they search. Some have accepted without question the role they must play. Deceived by the thought that the role and the man are one and the same, they comfort themselves with the philosophy, "That's the way life is."

This book is written to *you*. Not the "you" everyone knows, but the "little man inside" that for years you have supposed no one knew or ever would. God knows that man, understands him and loves him. At this point, I am not so interested in telling you what kind of person you are, as I am in helping you to discover *why* you are what you are. The effects I speak about must have a cause, and the greatest book known to man on the subject of human behaviour records it. That book is the Bible, God's precious Word. We know it is His Word because it tells the truth about us, and knows us as we are.

In the Bible, the first book, Genesis, is the book of beginnings. In it the origin of all things is found, and the peculiarities of the human personality are explained. You, as a person, are not merely the product of fate, nor the natural result of environment and training, but of nature. In Adam, your father, you will find the reason back of much of your behaviour. Each of us, his children, are really living in our own way his experiences in the Garden of Eden.

When God created Adam, He placed him in perfect surroundings—a beautiful garden, abundant food supply, pleasant circumstances and un-

2

limited possibilities of life. The whole earth was subject to him, and every living thing awaited his command. Blessed by God with a helpmeet (exact counterpart) named Eve to share his life, he enjoyed unbroken communion with her and with God. As he walked and talked with the Creator in the cool of the day, it was, indeed, paradise. Adam was *himself* with Eve and with God. Naked and not ashamed, he walked in quiet self-acceptance, resting in the undisputed fact that he was what he was by the grace of God. Resting in the wisdom and love of God, he saw himself as the expression of God's creation, hence known, understood and loved by both God and Eve.

All of this changed when Satan, through the serpent, cast the shadow of doubt upon the integrity of God; changed His truth into a lie; and accused Him of withholding good from Adam and Eve, hence causing them to doubt His love. The unbelief of their hearts was expressed in their act of disobedience, and so sin entered the human family; and spiritual death was the direct result. Death means separation—separation from God, and from each other—and the evidences of this death are plain to see in the events that followed.

The openness Adam and Eve had once enjoyed between themselves was gone. Their eyes were opened and they saw themselves as they were— naked—and they were ashamed of that nakedness. Self-acceptance turned into mutual rejection, and they busied themselves sewing fig leaves

3

together to hide their shame in each other's presence. The blessed liberty of "being themselves" with each other was gone, and they began to hide, revealing only that part of themselves they deemed worthy of acceptance. Judging what was good and evil in each other, they became actors wearing a mask; and the "little man inside" began his long, dreary exile.

In the cool of the day they heard God's voice; but instead of walking confidently and talking openly with Him, fear filled their hearts and they hid from His presence behind the trees in the garden. God's first word to Adam in his lost estate was in the form of a question: *"Where art thou?"*

Adam's children to this very day follow their father's practice of blaming others for their condition, hiding from God and one another, and never coming to grips with life's most important question. Ashamed of what and where we are, we go through life playing the hiding game, hiding from God and from one another. Wearing our self-made mask, we build walls about ourselves that keep others from the real person, and keep him inside. We cannot believe God loves us as we are; and so we begin a lifetime of performing in His presence, hoping to earn His acceptance. We cannot believe that man can accept and love us as we are, so in our shame we wear whatever leaves will please him, in hopes of earning his love and acceptance.

Our behaviour betrays the fact that the fall of

our father Adam left each of us with the basic emotional and spiritual problems that plagued him: fear, inferiority complex, and a haunting sense of guilt that seeks and finds relief only in hiding from man and God. Many and varied are the devices the human personality creates to cope with these basic needs, as any student of psychology will tell you. We ascribe technical terms and names to our problems in hopes of isolating them, thus helping us to cope with them. But when all our devices fail, we resort to Adam's way of escape—hiding. As we grow older, we call the "little man" feel true.

The hiding game begins early in life. As children we are open and honest with all we meet, just being ourselves without concern over self-acceptance. This is the sweet innocence that endears children to us. Without guile or deceit, they fully expose themselves to all, naked and unashamed in the presence of man. But soon they experience the first pains of rejection from others, and little by little begin to build their own world of unreality. Pressed into the demands of a society that forces unreal roles upon them in school, job and home, they retreat further and further into the silent world of nowhere. Adulthood arrives, and too often they find the outer man not true to the little man inside.

It is safe and secure in that prison. No one can hurt the real self, for he is never revealed to others. No one can reject him, for he is never offered to anyone. Only the image man, the masked actor playing his part, is ever seen and

Loneliness creeps in as the wall of prison gets thicker

known. All of this is fine, but sooner or later we make the discovery that we have taken into our hiding place a companion that none of us can live with forever. That companion is *loneliness*.

Loneliness was one of the effects of Adam's fall. He was alone in the beginning and God said it was not good for him to be alone, so He gave him as a precious gift, an helpmeet, Eve. Adam never knew loneliness in his perfect estate, but he and his children have lived with this destroyer ever since his fall. Adam knew loneliness the day he hid from Eve; for, doubting his acceptance as he was, he revealed only that part of himself he judged her willing to receive. Haunted by the realization that the image he projected was not true to the real man, the little man inside learned to live alone and lonely.

Another once wrote, "The whole conviction of my life now rests upon the belief that loneliness, far from being a rare and curious phenomenon, peculiar to myself and to a few other solitary men, is the central and inevitable fact of human existence." Loneliness creates an unbearable stalemate in most of us. Desperate to be known, accepted, understood and loved, we peer through the iron bars of our hiding places, daring at times to risk an exposure of our real selves, only to be greeted with hostility and rejection; and so we are driven deeper into ourselves.

We are like a timid flower who longs to unfold its beauty to the world, but is beset by frost and insects, develops a blight, clasps its petals firmly

6

to itself and hides its face from all. We search for someone who can be trusted with the revelation of ourselves without rejection, and listen with hope to the talk of love among mortals, only to find in experience that too often the only communication we are ever offered is mask to mask, not face to face.

So, shut up within, we live our quietly desperate lives. Our only companions are our fears, guilt, sense of inadequacy, and loneliness. Many times we are driven so deep within ourselves that we lose all hope of reality and all sense of personal identity. We search for medical, psychiatric, and spiritual answers and help, clinging only to the hope of survival for life. We say with sorrow, "There is no one I can talk to, for no one understands me."

Oh, timid soul, there *is* Someone Who knows you, understands you, and to whom you can tell all your heart and still He will love you! Please read on to the happy revelation of a God Who loves you *as* you are, and *where* you are; a God Who will be your Saviour and Friend in Jesus Christ, His Son!

The way of self-acceptance is to find acceptance with God. We need desperately to see ourselves — our true selves — through His eyes, accepted and loved as we are, if we are to be free. We will languish in our prisons forever if we wait for some human who will love us when we are unlovely, accept us when we are unacceptable, understand us when we are beyond human un-

7

derstanding. Only God, in Jesus Christ, can meet the needs of your heart. In His presence we can be what we are without fear . . . take off our mask; be freed from the need of man's acceptance; learn the glory of being alone without being lonely; and blossom in the sunshine of His love. In Him and His love we will discover our origin and destiny. Created to receive the revelation of His eternal love, we can find in Him the principle of our existence and its only end. To know the true power of His love in Jesus is to see earth metamorphosed; to live in the assurance of His love is to experience no winter or night—a life where all tragedies, dreary duties and fears vanish.

My immediate purpose is to assure you that there *is* Someone Who knows you as you are, and where you are. Never mind for now about your sins and failures. Please read on as He seeks to bring you under the banner of His love at Calvary's cross, where His forgiveness and provision for you were revealed. Let him fold you in His eternal love and acceptance, and set you free to walk with Him in the cool of the day in precious and real fellowship. Read in faith that God has found you and will speak to your deepest heart needs.

But in that, you can be freed from loneliness.

8

THE NEED OF LOVE

Visiting the state penitentiary as a chaplain, I was interested in the only entrance and exit to that dismal place. As I was led through a series of three massive gates, the system was explained. All gates were controlled by electronic devices and only one could be opened at a time. The gates were in the control of master switches that were carefully guarded.

The little man inside of each of us is in a similar place. Shut in by three massive gates with their iron bars, we languish in our prison of loneliness. These gates have already been mentioned as fear, inferiority complex, and a dreary sense of guilt within. These are the inescapable traits Adam passed on to each of us. As with all men in prison, many and ingenious are the methods we devise to open these gates. Shut away from others and from God, we endeavor to come up with some master plan that will unlock all three at once and set our weary personalities at liberty to be ourselves.

We imagine that assigning causes to our anxieties will better help us to cope with them. Hence, we have accepted the imagined reality of many phobias peculiar to us and hope this will help to free us. We apply the balm of self-confidence to our inferiority complex, but in spite of our bolstered attitude, we are often overcome by a sinking feeling of inadequacy—a sense of worthlessness that drives us further within ourselves. We establish rigid scruples by which we endeavor to regulate our behaviour in the hope that our haunting sense of guilt will be relieved by intermittent periods of self-acceptance.

If only every human soul could see that these unrelenting gates that imprison us are controlled by one master switch, and that by the finding of that key, all three can open at once and set the captive free! That master switch is LOVE. Your need is simply to experience *real* love.

"The greatest happiness in life is the conviction that we are loved; loved for ourselves — say rather, loved in spite of ourselves."

Lovelessness is the basic cause of all human misery. To live without love is to find no purpose, reason or plan for life, and our very existence becomes an empty, futile passage of time. The majority of our hospital beds are occupied by mental patients, those who are incapacitated because of crippling emotional and mental problems. Weary with trying to open the gates to freedom, they have given up to their prison and lost all contact with reality. The suicide rate in America is extremely high and is the third highest killer among the young people of our land. Yet, the answer to all their questions and solution to their problems in this life is to experience a real and lasting love. Most can relate to the sad words of Napoleon during the days of his exile, "No one ever loved me, not even my mother." Facing the inescapable reality of what he was, and remembering the empty gestures others made and called them love, made him conclude that there was no such thing as *real* love.

Though love has been the true subject of all poetry, music and philosophy, and the true moving force back of all human history and literature, the experience of real, true and lasting love has been as elusive as a shadow. Seldom do men grasp it so as to hold it. Love has been the object of all men's dreams, and without it life has no meaning. It has been defined a thousand times, and promised thousands more. It is the most sought after experience in life. Men have lived for it, suffered for it, died for it; yet seldom experienced it so as to satisfy and fulfill the great capacity of their heart for love.

Let us pursue this vast realm and see if, by God's help, we can discover a real and lasting love, a love that will open wide the gates that hold us and lead us into the liberty of life more abundant. We have searched for true love and been deceived; for we have searched among men, and men can love only themselves. Let us bring under the microscope the nature of love, and perhaps some of life's most frustrating questions may be answered.

Love is the key that will break
(1) fear, (2) inferiority complex, and (3) guilt
and free the "little man".

11

LOVE IS NOT LIKE

It has been said, "There is only one kind of love, but there are a thousand copies." It might be amended to read that there is but one real love, and as many copies as there are human beings in this world. The Bible simply declares, *"God is love."* Hence, there are as many concepts of love among men as there are concepts of God.

There are four words in the Greek language for "love." One of them has reference to the natural affection that is common to all life. It is almost like gravitation or some other blind force of nature, and is observed in animals as well as humans. Another word, *"eran,"* means only passion in its lowest form, seeking nothing but gratification, and is not found in the New Testament at all. Among the pagan Greek writers it was synonymous with sex love. The two remaining words are found to predominate the New Testament philosophy of love. One of them is the word *"phileo"* and its various forms, appearing around 45 times in all. Let me define this word, for in spite of the varied manifestations of love among mortals, all of them are based on this one concept.

It is the kind of love common to friends. It means to be fond of, or to have strong affection or personal attachment for another. It is an unimpassioned love that responds only to the pleasure it takes in a person or object. It is based on an inner community between the person loving and the person loved. Both have something in common. The one loving finds reflected in the person he loves, his own nature. This love is one of *liking*—an affection that is the outgoing delight to that which affords him pleasure. It is a non-ethical, mutual attraction that carries no obligation and makes no ethical demands on the person loving, as long as the person loved affords him pleasure. It demands no sacrifice from the one loving for the benefit of the one he loves. It is a reciprocal love, proper and legitimate. No standards of right or wrong are set by it as long as mutual pleasure exists; hence it is a love that loves those who are like themselves, and is, in the final analysis, *a love of self.*

In the New Testament it appears as the kind of love the world has for its own—the normal affection of a young woman for her husband and children; the normal affection of a child for his mother and father; the affection of a parent for his son or daughter. Judas expressed it for Jesus, and so did Peter. It is the common word to express the sentiments that exist between friends, and for our purpose here, we shall simply define it as a "performance love." I call it "performance love" for it must ever be stimulated or die. It must ever seek to earn and merit the love it gets in return. The enjoyment and return of it depends wholly on the excellency of our ability to perform to the satisfaction of the one who loves us.

We have all experienced the heartbreak of this kind of love. We thought we had found true love

13

at last, only to learn that when the moon went down, the music stopped, the flowers withered, the poetry had lost its magic, and our eloquent words of love ran out; the love we were sure would outlast time dissipated like the morning fog in the searing heat of the sun.

It is the only kind of love any of us have ever known outside the love of God in Jesus Christ. It is the kind of love that you first learned at your mother's knee. We were taught by precept and practice that if we were good boys and girls our parents and family would "love" us. We went to school to learn that the teacher "loved" good students and that, somehow, those who could not perform to her satisfaction were also shut out of the circle of her "love." In Sunday School we learned that "God loves good boys and girls," and our first concept of God was that the love He offered was regulated by our performance. We established the idea that "He will love me as long as I love and serve Him. When I fail, He will fail me. When I let down in my devotion and duty to Him, He will let me down." We thought of the love of God as a stern love that rewards good and punishes evil, or bad performance. We met this same kind of love when we learned that the employee who performed well came under the special "love" of his employer. Many have learned that this also is the true nature of most marital love. We have a phrase, "the honeymoon is over," meaning the era of time when failures, faults and inconsistencies in each other will no longer

14

be overlooked or tolerated. From now on each must perform to the satisfaction of the other in order to continue in the warmness of married love. No matter how much you may dislike this concept of love, you must admit that too often you have seen the tide of married love rise and fall in the exact proportions of your successful performance of your appointed or expected duties.

We are face to face with Adam's problem in the Garden of Eden. He must, in order to earn Eve's acceptance, show only that part of himself that is pleasing to her. The fig leaves must forever obscure the real Adam, for to show himself as he really was would mean certain rejection. His sense of inadequacy and heavy sense of guilt assured him that no other person could love him for what he was. His views were identical in regards to God. He must forever hide behind the trees and keep up with his daily performance in order to earn the right of God's love.

I have often seen this same kind of "love" offered in the professing Christian world as the Christian love of the New Testament. The Baptists love the Baptists as long as they are Baptists; the Methodist, Catholic, Presbyterian and all other sectarian love is of the same seamy material—a performance love that has nothing to do with God, but is in reality a selfish love of our own pleasure. You can remove Jesus Christ from the midst of most so-called Christian fellowship and their "love" would continue without interruption; for in reality, they only "love" those they "like."

The road of life is strewn with heartbreak and disappointment as a result of mistaking "like" for "love." Many a person has labored for years, faithfully performing his duties and obligations in the eyes of those he loves, to arrive at a time in life when he is no longer able to perform. It is here he learns with crushed heart that those who once said they "loved" him, now find no pleasure in him, and try as they will, can no longer conjure up the warm affections he had so long enjoyed.

Real love is what every man needs and yearns for. It is what our love songs are about, and what we have often believed ourselves to have attained, only to see it disintegrate under the friction of life.

Worldly love is "performance" dependent

REAL LOVE

There *is* a real love, a love that is beyond the power and grasp of mere men. Man cannot manufacture, buy, create, secure, hoard or destroy it. It is like manna from heaven, a daily blessing and pleasure sufficient for all our love needs but beyond our control. This real love must be bestowed as a free and permanent possession upon the heart, and must be revealed to the eyes of the inner man by faith. To say it is divine is to acknowledge the manifold mysteries of it. It is as impossible to comprehend with the reason as the infinite is to the finite mind. No song, or poem, or mere expression of words can tell its majesty or define its ecstasy. It probes deeper than mere fleshly pleasure; brushes the fortress of the mind away in a stroke; and plunges into the innermost recesses of the heart of the little man inside. It seeks only love, and is satisfied with only love in return.

It is a love that makes the unacceptable acceptable; loves what it does not like; never fails or withdraws itself; and continues for all eternity. *It is God's love for you!* It is a love so beyond human concepts that a new word was needed by the writers of the New Testament to convey the full grandeur of its nature. The word used throughout the New Testament for this love that I call "real love" is *"agapao,"* and appears 320 times in its various forms. This word is such a large

17

one that one translator said it required 35 English words to properly convey its meaning. One of the shorter translations gives this: *"A self-sacrificial love, called out of the heart due to the preciousness of the object loved."*

It is a love called out and bestowed freely upon the person loved by an awakened sense of value which causes the lover to prize him. It is the love of approbation and esteem—an impulsive love that recognizes the worth of its object, and this worth is in the heart of the lover. The beauty of its beloved is in the eye of the beholder and lover, and is a complete devotion on the lover's part. It is a love of ethical qualities, obligations, and responsibilities, and demands of the lover that he sacrifice himself for the benefit of the one he loves; love is not *real* unless it does. This kind of love has to do with the heart, and so directs the will, the mind and the reason. It has nothing whatever to do with the performance or lack of it on the part of the beloved; and in this fact alone lies the power of its unending nature.

The true and full definition of real love is given by the Apostle John: *"God is love."* It is not that God loves, but that He *is* love. Love is the expression of His personality corresponding to His nature. It is not a mere statement of His loving *action* toward you, nor of His tender *feelings* toward you, but of His true person. God, then, is the true source of all *real* love. Only those in whom He dwells can see another as God sees him, value him as God values him, and see what he may in Christ become.

In the Bible we are told that love flows from God, and that this love is "bestowed" upon us. Once bestowed, it is ours as a permanent possession and will never vary, nor will there ever be any shadow made by His turning in the direction of His love for us. Like the weather vane upon which the words were printed, "God is love" —no matter which way the wind blows, God still loves us. His love does not depend upon our performance of duty, but rests upon the faithful performance of His Son Jesus Christ. It is a self-sacrificial love that gave His beloved Son in our behalf, and so proved the genuineness of His love. His love is devoted to our eternal good and happiness, and can never end. In its bestowal it places upon its object a position, place, and nature that is not true to experience, and loves us in spite of the fact that we are not *now* what we *shall* be. He is dedicated to fashioning us into that which pleases Him, and never loses sight of what we shall eventually become because of His love.

To experience the love of God is to receive true boldness that will end fear, which has mental anguish, and replace it with confidence. We need never again fear to be ourselves with God or man. Our preciousness in His sight lies in the mystery of His love. His love is perfect, and so ministers perfect rest to our weary hearts. This love was bestowed upon us in spite of what we see or discover in ourselves. When we were and are without strength (unable to perform satisfactorily); ungodly (not like Him and opposed to His like-

19

ness); and sinners (enemies and violators of His commands), Christ died for us. This truly commends His love to us.

The love of God for us is impervious to all attacks of time and eternity. We are told that tribulation, distress, persecution, famine, nakedness, peril or sword shall have no effect upon it. His love for us shall conquer all, outlast all, withstand death, outlive angels, defeat principalities and powers; and nothing in the present, future or past shall ever diminish its fervor. It rolls over the endless attacks of earth and hell as the mighty sea rolls over the tiny sand castles built by the hands of naive children.

To experience the love of God in Christ is to know the patent influence of this love, guiding, directing, compelling the whole course of our lives. It compresses us forcibly by silken pressure into a new channel of life. It rules us without force or sword, and far from commanding, we are forced to obey it. The entire life is made anew, for a whole new man has been brought to life under the creative power of love. This love seeks always to lift us up and elevate us to a new response to His love, and desires through all eternity to show to others how much He loved us in Christ. It passes all knowledge in excellence, and to be filled with it is to be filled with the fullness of God. It recognizes all our imperfections without condemnation and labors in loving service to perfect us. His love never sees an opportunity but assumes a holy responsibility as it labors to cleanse, sanctify, and wash us from each spot, wrinkle and blemish. It nourishes, cherishes and loves us as Himself; and forsakes all that is dear to Himself to be joined to us forever. It is fervent and constant, and covers the multitude of our sins.

To know that we have been eternally accepted by God in spite of all He sees in us and knows about us, is the root and ground of abundant life. God-acceptance is the secret to self-acceptance, and the end of seeking acceptance in the sight of men. We are filled with confidence, our guilt is gone, our conscience purged, our fears cast out; perhaps alone, but never lonely, we are made well by the miracle of His love.

These few words about the nature of love are only to create in you a desire to know more about such wonderful love. It is my desire to now bring you fully into the presence of this love and press upon your heart the personal reality of it. May the Holy Spirit open your heart to these precious truths.

God's love is non-performance dependent
- Will abolish fear, inf. compx, & guilt

THE PROOF OF LOVE

Love words are cheap. Men use them lightly, promising eternal, undying love to those they seek to win. Millions of words have been written, sung and quoted to prove the reality of love. But God does not limit the revelation of His love for you to words. He declares that real love is not in words, nor of the tongue only, but in deed. Had He said a million times, "I love you," and had there been no deed of love, you would have every reason to doubt the genuineness of that love. He is willing to prove the sincerity of His love; rather, He is *anxious* to commend the nature of His love to you. He desires that His love be put on exhibit; that you be introduced to the wondrous nature of it and become convinced that God really loves *you!*

There is a time and place where He exhausted all means to demonstrate the great love wherewith He loved you. That place is the cross of Calvary, where His darling Son was given to death and hell in order that He might commend His love to you, accept and enjoy you. The scriptures tell that in the death of the Lord Jesus Christ, God manifested—that is, He caused to shine forth, made apparent—the eternal wonder of His love for you. There, in simple faith in the record God gave of His Son, you can perceive (that is, learn by experience and discernment) the truth of God's undying love for you.

Let me tell you the story of Jesus. My purpose is not to discourage you by endless scripture quotes as though I have something to prove to your reason; I have only a simple story of love to tell you. My ministry is to declare the record God has given of His Son to your needy heart in simple words you can receive as the Holy Spirit works the glory of faith in you.

The Eternal God was in the beginning, and with Him was His only begotten Son Who was the delight of His heart. In loving communion and fellowship they enjoyed each other's love by the power of their Holy Spirit. The Son was equal with the Father in all things, and never thought it robbery to be so. All things were created by the Son, and for His pleasure, and all heavenly creatures bowed before Him in glad worship and praise.

In the council halls of eternity, God foresaw the human race, and in that race He saw and knew you. For you He created the universe; allowed Lucifer to rebel against Him; purged the earth; planted a garden in Eden; created man in His image and allowed him to fall from his original estate to a place of alienation and separation. You were created to be the object of His affections, for God is love; and that love can only be manifested and God glorified as it is revealed to one who is unworthy of true love.

The mystery of His love to you was a secret hidden in the mind of God from before the foundation of the world, and was His original thought.

In holy counsel among the persons of the Godhead, it was predestined that one would come to earth in the fullness of time to tabernacle, or dwell temporarily, in the likeness of man in order to become like *you*, understand *you*, and to take your place at the judgment of God for your sin and sins. The Son took gladly this ministry of love; and there, in the presence of the holy angels, He wilfully laid aside the insignia of His majesty, all His divine and eternal rights as God, and came to earth to be born of a virgin that He might do the will of God, which was to bring *you* to Himself in love.

Bethlehem was not the origin of the Son of God. A woman bore the body He occupied, but the occupant was of old, from everlasting. He had walked the corridors of eternity; commanded the universe into existence; had given life to every living thing, and was Himself the light of the world He created. It was by His power that all things hung together, and all creation was subject to His eternal Word. A child was born that day at Bethlehem, but the eternal Son was a love gift from God. The Immanuel of the Old Testament prophecies had come—"God with us." The everlasting Father, the Prince of Peace, the eternal Counsellor, was the blessed darling Son of God whose very name would be called Wonderful.

The hands that had held back the seas had now become limited to the strength of man, and were made to cling to the finger of a woman. The eyes that were too holy to look upon sin were for a moment dimmed by the limited sight of a babe. The self-existent God was placed in dependence upon the earthly care of humans. He chose not to take upon Himself the nature of angels, but was for a season made lower than the angels that He might learn of you and the fellowship of your sufferings as a man. He who was rich became poor as a cringing beggar, that you through His poverty might become rich. So poor that a manger was His cradle; so helpless that He was carried in His mother's arms to the temple of God. He lived in obscurity, without wealth, influence or recognition. He rode to Jerusalem on a borrowed beast; He had no place to lay His head though the birds and foxes He made had the security of earthly shelter. His miracles are legend, and His words were unlike any words ever heard of man. He evidenced every proof of His divinity, yet lived within the limitations of man, depending only on the Holy Spirit of God for His help and strength.

From the day He entered the race He carried your sorrows and became by personal experience acquainted with all your grief. He was known for His many troubles and was called "man of sorrows." None ever saw Him laugh, but many saw Him weep as the dreary days went past under the heaviness of your lifetime of unhappiness. His only acquaintances were your griefs, and like a beast of burden, He bore them all without a murmur.

He suffered every sort of personal rejection.

25

He was despised, considered contemptible, judged the very last of all men, and in His death described Himself as *"a worm, and no man; a reproach of men, and despised of the people."* The race laughed and mocked Him to scorn when He sought to reveal Himself to them. He was rejected, left destitute of man, forsaken of all; and those who saw Him hid their faces from Him. He was afflicted, browbeaten of all; sinful men looked down their nose at such a despicable person; and though He was sorely depressed, He bore it all in silence, and like a lamb, remained silent as they led Him to the slaughter.

He was daily oppressed, that is, driven, taxed, harassed and tyranized. Those He came to save and love sought to ensnare and trap Him like a hunted animal. Pursued like a mighty army pursues a fleeing band of renegades; hounded as a debtor is browbeaten by his creditors, Jesus was the target of all the malice and hatred of the human heart for God.

He was the most misunderstood man of all history. Neighbors condemned His mother before He was born and He entered the race under a cloud of suspicion. In the eyes of men He never did a right thing in His life; it was wrong to be born in a manger if He was really the Son of God; wrong to desert His parents at the temple when He was 12 years old; wrong to live in Galilee, for no good thing ever came from such a wretched place. He was judged wrong by men to be eaten up with zeal for His Father's house. His words were wrong and all men sought to twist, pervert and warp every precious thing He uttered in hopes of trapping Him by His speech. They misunderstood His physical appearance and saw no beauty in Him at all. They considered His personal features so repulsive that they judged He had been smitten and afflicted of God to be so utterly void of beauty. He aged before His time under the load He carried for you. When He was but 30 years of age, the Pharisees estimated His age at near 50.

The wonderful miracles and works He performed for all were rejected as mere tricks and deception worked by the power of the Devil. His family and friends did not believe Him and He was condemned for doing good on the Sabbath, yet He was the Lord and fulfilment of the Sabbath. It was wrong to let a woman of the street touch Him in worship, and wrong to eat with sinners. It was wrong for Him to enter the house of a wicked man like Zacchaeus, and if He was really God it was wrong to have harlots and sinners as His friends. Who ever heard of a king riding upon a donkey, or entering his capital city without heralds and an impressive army? Even Peter, the spokesman of the apostles, rebuked Him publicly for the mere mention of His purpose to die at Calvary for you.

He was the only Life mankind had ever known, yet they comprehended it not. He was the true Light that came to light every man, yet men He made gave Him no recognition. He came to save men and enable them to be the sons of God, yet they would not associate themselves with Him in a personal and intimate way. He walked all the lonely years of His life misunderstood and in the form of a slave, and died a man of no reputation. He was truly the Lamb of God, and as a Lamb He was shorn in His silence and slaughtered in His meekness; betrayed by one who had lifted his hand in fellowship with Him at the last supper; denied by the one man who had once declared Him truly to be the Son of God; hated by the nation He chose from among all nations to be His very own.

Listen with your heart as I tell you how He crossed the brook Kidron, east of Jerusalem, on the last night of His hell on earth. There where the ground slopes upward to the Mount of Olivet He enters a garden known as Gethsemane, in the pale light of a full moon, with the smell of spring in the air, and He falls on His face in the agony of prayer. Terror fills His heart—shock and amazement overtake Him; with heart pounding, throat dry, this once peaceful and happy man who had just sung a hymn of praise and spoken cheerfully of His approaching death, now bursts into tears. Sweat now stands out on that lovely face, and it appears to be as blood.

What turned His communion to separation . . . His peace to trouble . . . His joy to grief? It was something that He saw in that place of prayer. It was not the full impact of what Judas had done, nor was it the experiences of the night yet ahead of Him, nor the fear of the cross with its nails and spear. It was something offered to Him by His Father. He said it was a *cup*; and dear reader, your sins, iniquities, transgressions, and all the guilt, penalty, rejection and death that belongs to *you*, filled that cup. It was offered to Him to take as His very own and to drain in His death at Calvary. This is what He thirsted for, and this is what He finished at the place called Golgotha. No wonder He was heavy, depressed and confused as one not at home and in unfamiliar circumstances. No wonder He was exceeding sorrowful, encompassed with grief and encircled in an ocean of sorrow. No wonder that it almost killed Him and in His agony caused Him to pray,

"O my Father, if it be possible, let this cup pass from me: nevertheless not as I will, but as thou wilt."

Hear Him give now the death wail—a sharp, shrill, ear-piercing shriek followed by prolonged wails and sobbing—as He sees for the first time the full price He must pay for your acceptance.

He came to earth to commend His love to *you*. He came to earth to prove the sincerity of that love. He came to earth, and to this moment, to take away forever from your heart the doubt that *God loves you.* He saw the cost of that love and the sacrifice it would demand. He saw the impossibility of saving you without the cross and the hell He must take for you. It was *you*, dear reader, who turned the most precious earthly place of fellowship and communion into a living hell. It was *you* who would separate Him from

His Father's face; *you* who nearly killed Him that night as He looked into your heart and life and saw you as you are. But oh, dear reader, Jesus having loved you, loved you to the very end.

They take Him away now. The longest night on earth has begun for Jesus. They accuse Him, condemn Him, tie His blessed hands and smite Him with their fists in the face until He is beyond human recognition. They lash Him with a cruel lash into whose leather thongs bits of glass and metal have been embedded to create a pattern of brutality across His precious back that resembles a freshly furrowed field. They make for the King of Glory a crown woven from the acacia bush with thorns as long as a man's finger and sharp as a needle. They pierce His brow, spit upon Him, curse and mock Him throughout the long night, and lay upon His bleeding back the cross upon which He will hang. Taunted and driven like a criminal, He struggles along the path of sorrows until He falls beneath His load, exhausted. He is dragged to Calvary, spread-eagled on the cross, nails driven through the hands and feet, lifted up between heaven and earth, the cross thumped into the socket of rock to wrench every bone out of place.

And now the true dimensions of God's love can at last be revealed. It is here at the cross, not in His earthly life, that God's love is fully manifested to you. Here is where true love will not fail—will hang on and never let go until He has proven the sincerity of that love for *you*, the little man inside.

Here at the crossroads of eternity God is at His best and man is at his worst. See yourself in the self-righteous people who jeer, curse, mock and spit upon Him. See yourself, for had you been there you would have joined them. See yourself in the Jews, too sensitive to touch a corpse, concerned about removing Him from the tree before sundown that they might go to their ritual on the morrow with clean hands. See them scurrying like rats to Pilate to beg him to allow soldiers to take a heavy wooden mallet and break His legs to be sure He dies quickly. See the soldiers come to find that He is dead already. One look at His face with the matted beard stained with blood, sweat and tears for you, tells them He is dead. They had heard His cry, *"My God, my God, why hast thou forsaken me?"* Now they take a large spear and open His side with a wound so large that later Thomas could have placed his hand into it, and from that wound comes gushing forth a fountain of blood and water.

There is something wonderful about that incident. John describes it in his gospel as though he were extremely anxious for us to know that it is of great importance that we believe his record. The centurion was so amazed by the manner of His death that he believed Him to be a righteous man and declared Him to be the Son of God.

Jesus did not have to die. He said before He went to the cross that He was like a corn of wheat that had fallen into the earth (mankind). If He died He would bring forth fruit; if He did not die,

He would abide alone. He wanted you so much— He loved you so intensely, He gladly and joyfully died of His own free will. He said no man could take His life from Him, and that He would lay it down Himself. At the cross He dismissed His Spirit and gave up the ghost of His own volition. He is the only man who ever died by his own will. He did not suffer death; it was a free dying, an act of His own will for *you*!

Many and varied are the theories given for the medical cause of Jesus' death. Let me give you my thoughts. Under intense mental and emotional anxiety, a sudden rupture of the heart is possible. Surrounding the heart is a membrane or sac, called the pericardium, containing water-like substance. Its purpose is to lubricate the heart's surface in its continual motion. When the heart ruptures, blood often rushes into the pericardium and separates into its two substances, blood and water. If this is true in the case of Jesus, the sac fully extended, once pierced by the spear, would instantly release its contents. Hence the stream of water mixed with clotted blood which issued from His blessed side was the external evidence of the real cause of His death.

He was not killed by the Jews, nor by the Romans, nor by the lash, the crown or the fists of men. The nails did not take His life, nor did exhaustion or any other sort of physical suffering. He gave up to the burden He carried for *you*, and the travail of His soul for *you* killed Him. *You broke the Saviour's heart!* This heartbreak He carried to Calvary, and for which He sacrificed His life, began in Eden when you in your father Adam were separated from God and doubted His eternal love for you.

"To have been the cup His lips touched and blessed,
To have been the bread which He broke;
To have been the cloth He held as He served,
Or the water He poured as He spoke.

"To have been the road He walked on the way,
To have been His print in the sand;
To have been the door that opened the tomb,
But you were a nail in His hand!"

But wait . . . this is not the end of the story of Jesus and God's great love for you. Jesus died for the unjust that He might bring them to God. He died a *substitutionary* death. He literally took your place in death that you might take His place in life. You have looked at the earthly view of the cross . . . now see heaven's view.

God is holy and you are unholy. God is righteous and you are unrighteous. God is pure and you are defiled. God declared the wages of your sin to be death—not merely physical death as Jesus suffered at the cross, but separation from God in outer darkness for all eternity; for no unclean person can stand in the presence of a holy and pure God. When Jesus died, God counted you to be in Him. He called you into His presence in judgment, and imputed your sins and iniquities to Christ Himself. This is why God forsook Him at death. He dared to approach God clothed in the filthy rags of your righteousnesses, and God banned Him from His presence. God refused to deal leniently with Him, though He was His beloved Son, but delivered Him up to the outer darkness for you. Jesus could not enter heaven clothed in your sin.

The Word of God declares how He went into the lower parts of the earth and visited the hell you deserved. He descended into the pit, and carried to that place of banishment your sins, and all that would have separated you from God forever. God so loved you that He gladly gave up His Son for you; and Jesus so loved you that He would not let you go, even though it meant the pains of death and the horrors of hell.

But hell had no claim on the Saviour. He was not a *sinner,* but a *sin bearer* for you; and as such, could not be held in that place. God raised Him from among the dead ones and brought Him to paradise to meet the thief He saved while on the cross; and there for three days and nights He announced the good news to the Old Testament saints that God's love had opened heaven's gate for all sinners who rest in that perfect love. He entered heaven on the day of the resurrection and took with Him the blood of His sacrifice and the first fruits of His victory, presented them to God and was seated at His right hand. God glorified Him with the glory He had before the foundation

34

of the world and gave Him a name that is above every name in heaven, on earth or beneath the earth. There at the right hand of God's eternal throne the blessed Son of Man sits, His work complete; God's love demonstrated; heaven opened for you, the guilty sinner; and the eternal Godhead glorified forever.

They say that "time heals all wounds," but here is the eternal denial of that maxim. The wounds of Jesus will never heal. They remain today as the everlasting reminders of how much God loves *you*. He was wounded for *your* transgressions, and bruised for *your* iniquities; and even though a mother may forget her sucking child, He will never forget *you* nor let you forget, for He has graven you on the palms of His hands. Never speak of the nail-scarred hands of the Saviour. Those wounds are still as fresh as though He were slain this moment, that God's compassions for you might be new each morning of your life, and His great faithfulness demonstrated in loving you without waiting for you to perform to His satisfaction. He is fully satisfied in the death of the Son, and all His demands and requirements have been silenced forever in those precious wounds. When Jesus comes back to earth in glory the Jewish nation will ask Him, *"What are these wounds in thine hands?"* and He will tell them that they were made in the house of His friends.

You are fully forgiven and loved for His name's sake alone. Not anything you have done, will do, or are doing now will ever establish any other relationship with God. He did all this for you when you were without strength (unable to perform); ungodly (not like Him, and what He did not like); a sinner (enemy); and hostile to the blessed God Who loves you. He has freely bestowed this love upon you as a permanent possession, and He loves you without any merit on your part.

Lay hold of this precious love by faith and you will never hide from God or man again. *God loves you! Jesus died for you!* Who can be against you? No charge can ever be laid against you in His sight. He has fully justified you on the grounds of Jesus Christ's finished work. His blood has washed you white as snow in the sight of God. His love will make you whole; free you from a lifetime of guilt, fears, inferiority complex and dreary loneliness; and open wide the gates that long have imprisoned you. It is nothing you have done. It is the precious blood of Christ that even now cleanses you continually from all manner of sin and sins. His blood is your present and eternal peace, hope and righteousness. What a precious fountain for uncleanness!

God has accepted you in the beloved Son — what need have you to grovel at the feet of men, ever performing to win their fleeting acceptance and favor? What need have you ever again to fear to be yourself? — God loves you as you are! How shall you ever be lonely when He Himself is with you, and will be with you as long as the precious eternal blood of His Lamb is on the mercy seat in heaven for you? At last you can walk with Him without shame, and walk with men in the reality of what you are. Your days will be cool, and God will be your Friend; and perhaps you will enjoy a little of paradise while still on this earth.

—Can't be summed up   Read it.

THE RESPONSE OF LOVE

The record of God concerning His great love for us is so marvelous, so overwhelming it fills our hearts with wonder. Surely if we are ever to perceive real love, it is at the cross. There He commends the infinite nature of it and proves beyond question its sincerity. But the little man inside of you has hidden so long from God that it is difficult to really believe it was all for him. You have lived so long afraid to even think that someone could love you, let alone God Himself. Most of us have been intimidated by the impersonal words of modern evangelism that stress the love of God for "mankind." It is true that *"God so loved the* world, *that He gave his only begotten Son, that* whosoever *believeth in him should not perish, but have everlasting life."* Perhaps these broad terms discourage and defeat you, but listen with your heart as I tell you that the cross was for *you* alone.

The Apostle Paul prayed that you might be able to comprehend the breadth, and length, and depth, and height, and to know by deep personal experience the love of Christ for you. He longed that you would be rooted and grounded in this marvelous fact, that God loves *you*, and proved it by sending His Son to die. Paul himself had a deep personal knowledge of Jesus' love for him. When he spoke of the cross he said Christ loved *him* and gave himself for *him*. He never thought in terms of the world, but when He saw Calvary, he saw only Jesus and himself.

The eternal love wherewith God loved you is a self-sacrificial love called out of His great heart, due to the preciousness of the object loved. That object was *you*. It was *you* who called out of His great heart the love that sent His only begotten Son. It was *you* who called out of the heart of Jesus in Gethsemane the willingness to take the cup of your sin and sins and drain its bitter dregs at Calvary. It was *you* who worked the pressure of love within His breast that caused Him to suffer the separation of your spiritual death.

You are not just one soul among millions for whom He died. Had there been no other human being on earth, the history of the cross would remain unchanged. Had the eternal record of mankind contained but one name, and that name *yours,* Jesus would still have left heaven to die in your stead. He knew *you* before the foundation of the world, and His eternal eyes saw only *you* from His blessed home in glory; and the preciousness of the one He saw drew Him to Calvary to give Himself for *you*.

There is not another person in the world like you in His sight. You are unique, for He made you so. He not only created you, but formed you as a potter shapes a vessel for himself. He made you as you are, that you might receive the personal revelation of His love for you, and that He might enjoy the privilege of loving *you*. All your beauty

is in His eye, and your loveliness is in the heart
of the blessed lover of your soul. Your eternal
worth and preciousness can only be explained in
the mystery of this great fact: *"God is love."*

But all your experience with love in this life
has been with a "performance" type of love. All
who ever said before, "I love you," demanded that
you do something in return to earn that love; and
so perhaps even now you are asking, "What must
I *do* to be saved? What am I expected to believe?
What performance will God expect and demand of
me in view of His love to me?"

Dear reader, hear this good news—God only
wants you to *love him!* This is the only response
He wants of you, and is the real evidence of saving
faith. Difficult and confusing are the explanations
theologians give when asked what it really means
to believe to the saving of the soul. They prattle
on about doctrine, dogmas and creeds as though
saving faith were a matter of intellectual consent
to a religious philosophy. The essence of real
saving faith and the inner assurance of salvation
is simply discovering that we have fallen in love
with Jesus, because He first loved us!

True and real love, as seen in the cross, begets
love in the heart of the one who believes. Love
is the Holy Spirit's witness to the reality of true
faith. Peter once stood before a crowd and confessed his faith in the doctrine of Christ by de-
claring,

*"Thou art the Christ, the Son of the living
God."*

The demons knew as much and trembled in the reality of their knowledge. Later this same man, under satanic pressure, denied with an oath the very Lord He had confessed. After the resurrection Jesus met Peter at the shore of Galilee and asked him a deep, searching, personal question, *"Lovest thou me?"* He did not ask Peter what he believed, but what he knew and felt in his heart toward Jesus Himself. This was after Peter had been to Calvary and watched Him die. This was after Peter had seen the wounds in His hands and side, and had discovered that Jesus bore his sins in His own body on the tree. Now, after proving beyond question *His* love for Peter, He has every right to ask Peter what he feels in his heart for Himself. Jesus longs only to hear him say, "I love you."

Peter cannot look at his performance for his answer, for it had been very bad. He cannot look at his faithfulness for an answer, for he had failed the Lord. He cannot look at others for assurance, for they had been led away from Jesus by Peter himself. He cannot look at the past for it is filled with nakedness, fear, guilt and an overwhelming evidence of inadequacy. He dare not look at tomorrow, for he had learned the weakness of his flesh and his inability to do what he knew was right. Peter can only look at Jesus' hands and side, marked with the eternal evidences of His undying love for Peter *as he was,* and answer honestly out of the depths of his heart,

"Lord, thou knowest all things; thou knowest that I love thee."

41

This love was not something Peter *did*, but something he could not *help* doing.

The boldness of Peter's answer must have shocked him. Naked, guilty, worthless, ashamed of the black record of his denial in the judgment hall, yet in spite of all he was and had discovered so recently about himself, he loved Jesus from the depth of his heart and could not deny it. Jesus knew Peter loved Him; He wanted Peter to know that this was all He asked. God is not asking you if you understand the theology of the cross, or if you can explain the details of Jesus' sacrificial death for you. He is asking you to look within your heart and answer honestly whether or not His love has begotten in you a love for Himself. Never mind for now about your duties as a Christian; this is your first duty, and in loving Him because He first loved you, all duties will find their proper performance.

All words employed in the Bible that express what the sinner is to "do" in order to be saved are fully explained by one word: *love.* You cannot believe in a person without loving him. You cannot really trust yourself to another unless you love him. You cannot receive a person to your heart without loving him. Love is faith experienced in the heart, and is the Holy Spirit's proof to you that you are a believer. Only the Holy Spirit can enable you to love Jesus. No man can call Him Lord but by the Holy Ghost. When Paul wrote to the early Christians he sent his greetings only to those who loved our Lord Jesus Christ in sincerity. Not to all those who confessed the Christian creed; who attended the assembly; who had done Christian works and proven themselves faithful—but to those who were believers in fact and were known by this single mark: they loved Jesus Christ sincerely. Those who are the called of God according to His purpose are those who love God.

To love the Lord with all our heart, and soul, and mind, is the first and great commandment of the law. All the law and prophets hang on this one reality. Loving Jesus Christ is doing more than all the sacrifices and offerings of the law; it is greater than tongues, gifts, works, benevolence or martyrdom. It is that which fulfils every law God ever gave and performs every duty He ever placed before men. When we learn that we do not have to perform to be loved, for the first time we find ourselves wanting to perform for the joy of Him Who loves us. Love is the only debt we owe Him; and when faith, hope and all other Christian graces are vanished, love will remain.

The love of God bestowed on you in Jesus Christ finds its fulfilment in the response of your heart. He demands nothing, seeks nothing but that you love Him. Let me ask you now—do you love Jesus Christ? Not do you serve Him faithfully, read your Bible, pray, witness, attend church, give, perform Christian works—*do you love Him*? If you are a true believer this is the one thing you cannot deny. In spite of all you see and discover daily about your poor wretched heart, that one blessed reality remains. I trust that you can sing from your heart the sweet words of that hymn:

"My Jesus, I love Thee, I know Thou art mine,
  My Rock and my Fortress, my Surety divine;
My gracious Redeemer, my Saviour art Thou,
  If ever I loved Thee, my Jesus, 'tis now.

"I love Thee because Thou hast first loved me,
  And purchased my pardon on Calvary's tree;
I love Thee for wearing the thorns on Thy brow,
  If ever I loved Thee, my Jesus, 'tis now."

Perhaps you are saying, "I *do* love Jesus, but I do not love Him as much as I should, or not nearly as much as others." Hush! Listen to me! When Peter answered our dear Lord's question, he could only honestly define his love as weak and less than self-sacrificial. John was the apostle of love, a deep, fervent lover of Jesus; but Jesus did not ask Peter to love Him as much as John loved Him. There are no degrees of love. He does not measure your love on a scale to determine its reality. Your love is unique because you are unique. No one can love Jesus with the love you have to give Him. Jesus is satisfied with the little or much of your love, for it is called out of your heart by His preciousness. Each day of your life He will become more precious to you than ever before, as you learn more of how very much He has forgiven you. The woman who came to Jesus while He ate with Simon the Pharisee, to break the alabaster box of precious ointment, anoint His feet, weep over Him and wipe His feet with her long hair (her glory), did so because she loved Him much. Jesus said her great love was due to her deep sense of having been forgiven much. The much that you have been forgiven will be unfolded a day at a time to your heart. As you discover more about yourself, you will discover more of the dimensions of His love, and so the sense of your own love for Him will deepen proportionately. Do not try to imitate another's love for Jesus. *Your* love is important to Him, for no other can love Him as you do.

If someone were to ask a father, "Which of your children do you love the most?" he would answer, "I love each one differently, for they are different persons, and each one calls from my heart a unique kind of love." This love belongs to each child exclusively, and each expression of love from each child is unique and precious. So with Jesus, dear reader. The little or the much of your love for Him is the personal expression of your own unique heart and is precious to His. Hear Him now as He asks only to see the travail of His soul at Calvary—*"Lovest thou ME?"* May each of us answer Him in these words:

"I love Thee, Lord, but with no love of mine,
For I have none to give;

45

I love Thee, Lord, but all the love is thine,
   For by Thy love I live;
I am as nothing, and rejoice to be
   Emptied, and lost, and swallowed up in
   Thee."

God asks only one thing; love.

Not Demands

THE ASSURANCE OF LOVE

The Apostle John wrote:

"Behold, what manner of love the Father hath bestowed upon us, that we should be called the sons of God . . . "

The word "manner" means "what sort or quality," and is from a root word which implies "what country, tribe or race." So John marvels at the foreign, unearthly, other-worldly quality of God's love for us. Surely we have never seen this kind of love apart from His! To know that He has bestowed this love as a permanent possession upon such unworthy persons as we are, and has called us, or named and confessed us, as His sons, is earth's greatest knowledge.

Paul describes it as the riches of God's glory that will make you strong in the little man inside. Jesus Christ dwelling in your heart by faith will securely and deeply settle you, and will enable you to take eagerly for yourself a greater confidence in the limitless dimensions of His love. You will progressively learn by your daily experience with Him the eternal security of His love for you, and earth's knowledge will fade into insignificance as He fills you with the fullness of Himself.

All your heart needs are met in the perfect love of God for you. God is *for* you. Who can set themselves against you with any success? He will freely give you all things that are for your good and His glory. He has made you His personal concern and you may confidently cast upon Him all your anxieties or worries. He has endowed you with love, and so with Himself. Your daily confidence in the unearthly nature of His love will wipe out all sense of time, destroy all memory of a beginning, and all fears will be brought to an end. This gift of His love in Jesus Christ is good and perfect, and has come to you from the Father of lights Whose very nature assures you of no variableness, and whose gifts and callings are without repentance.

You are fully accepted by Him as you are, for He accepts you in the person of His beloved Son. As God clothed Adam in a coat of skin, taken from one who gave his life that Adam might walk unashamed and acceptable, He has clothed you in the perfect righteousness of Himself. He will never condemn, criticize or shame you. Reconciled forever to God by the merits of Jesus Christ, you may enjoy perfect peace as you face Him. He is fully satisfied with the sacrifice of Christ Who even now is at the right hand of God making intercession for you. His love will never fail, or fall away, or be driven out of its determined course to make you what you are not now—like Himself.

As you reflect on His perfect love, you will enjoy increasing boldness even at the thought of judgment; for as He is now, so are you. Fear shall be turned away from the door of your heart and its mental anguish ended. His love exists in

His own nature, and no daily discovery about yourself will ever discourage Him, for He first loved you. He will never cease to sustain and uphold you. He will never let you down, leave you in the lurch, or abandon you. You may boldly say that the Lord is your helper, and you need not ever fear what any man might seek to do to you.

The Lord, the self-existent, eternal *"I am,"* Who created and formed you to receive the revelation of His love, has redeemed you. He has called you by your name and you are His. When you pass through the waters of life, they will not overflow you; when you walk through the fire of trial and test, you will not be burned, nor shall the flame ever kindle upon you. The Holy One is your Saviour in life and death, and has already given His beloved Son for your ransom. Rejoice, dear reader; you are precious in His sight! No matter how you may appear in your own sight or in the sight of others, He sees in you what no man can see, and calls you precious, for He sees what His love shall make you. He loves you, and will give whatever is needed for you in this life, so let not your heart be troubled or afraid; He is with you. He created you for His glory, and He will not let you go until all creation praises Him as they behold His glory reflected in you.

> *"O love that wilt not let me go,*
> *I rest my weary soul in Thee;*
> *I give Thee back the life I owe,*
> *That in Thine ocean depths its flow*
> *May richer, fuller be."*

I have often likened the Christian's experience to the story of Lazarus. Jesus loved Lazarus, though he was sick and ultimately died. It seems strange that when Jesus first hears of Lazarus' illness He makes no hurried effort to reach him, but calmly waits until the news arrives that Lazarus is dead. Arriving in Bethany four days later, He finds him already buried and by this time smelling very bad. Wrapped in grave clothes, with a linen napkin covering his face, he is hidden forever from the eyes of the world. Jesus was glorified in the eyes of all who beheld the miracle of resurrection as Lazarus came forth by the power of the Word of God in newness of life. But that is not the end of Jesus' work. There is the command that follows the giving of life: *"Loose him and let him go."* His hands and feet are still bound with the grave clothes and his face, his real likeness, hidden by the napkin he had worn in death. Jesus' desire is that now he will be loosed to walk with Him, use his hands for His glory, and show his real face to all.

The outward transformation of the Christian life is the release of the little man inside. It is the metamorphosis that comes to pass when we learn with the heart that God has accepted us as we are, and that we no longer need to hide from Him or one another. Set at liberty to be ourselves with God and man, the freedom we may experience regains a little of the paradise lost. This same thought is implied in the very words used in the Hebrew and Greek words of the Bible that are translated "salvation." The ideas of deliverance, safety, preservation, healing, and soundness are all found in these words. Accepted eternally by the Father, we are safe forever by the precious blood of Christ. Preserved in Jesus Christ and destined to wear the glory, we have been delivered from the wrath to come. From the moment we receive His love for us in saving faith, there is a healing process begun. Soundness of the whole man begins to appear as we slowly learn to walk in the reality of His love and grace. Like a flower exposed to the warmth of the sun, the petals slowly unfold to reveal more and more of the beauty of the little man inside, as the preciousness of the Lord Jesus Christ fashions him into His own likeness.

The next appearance of Lazarus in the Gospel narrative following Jesus' command to *"Loose him and let him go"* finds him in sweet fellowship with Jesus. As he sits at supper with Jesus, enjoying His presence without fear or shame, many people of the Jews heard about the miracle and came to see for themselves. They did not come only to see Jesus; they came also to see the man who was dead, now very much alive and loosed from his tomb to be himself with God and man. Jesus had not only become Lazarus' Saviour from death, but was also his Friend for life.

Dear reader, you have a lifelong Friend in Jesus—one with Whom you can at last be just what you are and know that He will continue to love and accept you. What happy days are ahead for you! There is no need to hide anything from Him, for He has seen the very worst already. If the stench of your death and the sealed tomb that once held you did not discourage Him in the past, the future is filled with the joy of His continued fellowship and love.

After salvation, God desires fellowship.

THE FRIENDSHIP OF LOVE

You must never think of yourself in the presence of God apart from Jesus Christ. Being justified by faith, you have eternal peace facing God. That peace is a blessed Person—Jesus Christ Himself. He has been made both peace and perfect righteousness for you. You were crucified, buried, and raised again in newness of life with Him, and are now seated in Him at the right hand of God's eternal throne. Jesus Christ is your Advocate facing the Father, and is now called alongside to help you. His precious blood has completely satisfied God forever; and your everlasting acceptance is assured by His never ending life.

While all of this is wonderfully true for those who have believed and bear the evidence of real faith, which is an undeniable love in their hearts for Christ, there is another side to this blessed truth. We are still here upon the earth facing the reality of life in the often undesirable and unbearable circumstances in which we find ourselves. Never think of yourself in life apart from the reality of His presence. Though He is present at the throne in His resurrected body of flesh and bone, He is also dwelling in your heart by faith; and He longs to make His presence a reality to you.

How little most persons know by experience of His abiding presence! Knowing Him as *Saviour* seems to suffice; but He longs to manifest Himself to us in our daily walk and be our dearest *Friend*. Though Jesus was never seen on earth after His ascension into heaven at the Mount of Olivet, His unseen presence was a constant reality to the early believers. He had promised at His departure to be with them, and us, always, even to the end of the age. He assured us He would never leave us nor forsake us. Christ dwelling with and in us was to be the hope of our glory and also of His. He said He would not leave us comfortless, or like orphaned children, but would come to us. He said that if we loved Him, His Father would love us, and He Himself would love us and reveal or manifest Himself to us. When questioned as to how such a miracle would take place, He answered that He and His Father would come and take up their abode, or permanent dwelling place, with us. This, He assured us, would give us a precious peace like He Himself had enjoyed on earth, and we would never need to let our hearts be troubled or afraid.

This was wonderfully true in the lives of the first Christians. Somehow we are prone to delegate this reality to the first century; but dear reader, it is just as true for you today! Jesus walked the dusty road of life with the Emmaus disciples, though their hearts were filled with unbelief, and though they accused Him of being a stranger to where they were and indifferent to their hearts' needs. They could not see Him, did not recognize His voice, and looked to each other for answers to their questions and solutions to their problems.

None of this discouraged Him from overtaking them in their gloomy walk and patiently talking with them, until their eyes were opened once more to the reality of His presence with them, and their hearts were set on fire by His love.

On the resurrection morning Peter and John busied themselves with trying to unravel the *mystery* of His resurrection, while Mary Magdalene longed only for the reality of His *presence.* She was not disappointed, for Jesus made His presence known to her; He spoke her name in love and made her to know that she was not alone in the confusion of life. He revealed Himself to the women at the tomb that day, and sent them to tell the other believers that He would go before them in the road of life and they would see Him again. His presence was a reality to Paul in the Philippian jail; Jesus talked with him and filled his heart with praise. Later, as Paul sat in another jail cell, he wrote his epistle of joy to the Philippians to assure them that the personal presence of Jesus was still as real as ever, for he wrote, *"The Lord is at hand!"* In his final trial at Rome that ended in his death, he testified that though no man stood with him and all had forsaken him, the Lord Jesus stood with him and strengthened him. The disciples in Jerusalem had quiet confidence through their persecutions, and observers could not deny that their courage came because they had been with Jesus.

Jesus wants to be that real to you. He longs to manifest Himself as your one true Friend in this life. So many of us look constantly to and seek the friendship of others; we consult them, desire their comfort and fellowship and walk gloomily along, ignoring the ever present Friend that sticketh closer than a brother.

Nothing in this world is of higher esteem or value than a true friend—another self, as it were, to whom we can impart our secret thoughts, who partakes of our joy and comforts us in our afflictions; one whose company is an everlasting pleasure; one person whom we can utterly trust with ourselves, who knows the best and worst of us and loves us in spite of our faults; someone with whom we can talk face to face without shame, fear, guilt or pretence and be assured that he will love us in spite of all he sees. An old Arabian proverb puts it this way:

"Friendship is the comfort, the inexpressible comfort of feeling safe with a person, having neither to weigh thoughts nor measure words, but pouring all right out just as they are, chaff and grain together, certain that a faithful friendly hand will take and sift them, keep what is worth keeping, and with a breath of comfort, blow the rest away."

You *have* such a friend; His name is Jesus! I pray that the reality of His friendship will be your experience.

In the Bible there is the story of a man who walked with God. His name was Enoch. He possessed the witness in his heart that his walk pleased God; and the thing about Enoch that pleased the Lord so much was that he daily came to God believing that He would walk with him, and diligently sought the reality of His presence. Enoch was rewarded abundantly with the sweet fellowship of God's Person.

When I first became a Christian I also knew the blessedness of such a walk with Jesus. He was as real to me as humans around me, and I practiced daily the presence of the Lord. I talked with Him as I drove my car, communed with Him as I trudged along horseback to my mountain churches, listened to Him in the night as He gave me songs of praise; I told Him about my burdens and fears, and consulted with Him about my activities and plans. Over the years some of this preciousness was lost as I turned more to men than to Him. I found it easier, or so I thought, to discuss my needs with men than with Him. Loneliness was a constant companion until I rediscovered the reality of His friendship. This was worked by the continual failure of men to be what *He* longed to be to me. I found human friendships fleeting and faulty. I realized the impossibility of another human understanding me. I saw the futility of a man bearing the full sight of what I really was within, without rejection and misunderstanding. In my desperate need I was driven to Jesus in the realization that if He were not my Friend, then earth was desolate, and life empty and futile. He did not disappoint me! He had *always* been there, and revealed Himself again to my needy heart. I share this testimony with you in hope that it will encourage you to remember what a Friend you have in Jesus.

Let me do as the little maid in the Song of Solomon and tell you about my Beloved Who is altogether lovely, and Who is my Friend.

Jesus will be your Friend, who will always be w/ you.

THE UNDERSTANDING OF LOVE

Jesus is the only friend you will ever have who totally understands you. No matter how diligently you endeavor to explain to others how you think or feel, they are limited in their understanding. First, it is impossible for others to be objective enough in their understanding; and next, they cannot know the varied pressures, emotions, motives and impulses that cause you to act and react as you do. Your personality is unique, and no other human on earth can fully grasp the many facets of your make-up. Jesus understands you fully because He made you. The Word of God declares that by the Lord Jesus Christ *all* things were created, and He is the source of their life. You were created by Him, and for Him; and we are also told that He formed you. This means that He determined your shape as a potter determines and shapes a vessel to his pleasure. You are not the result of accident or fate, but of design. He knows more about you than you know yourself, and understands all the peculiarities of your personality.

The Word of God also tells us that He, in His incarnation, was made like unto His brethren, or those who would be a part of His Father's family by faith in the beloved Son. Which one of His brethren do you suppose He was made like? He was made like *you*, that He might understand you and become your dearest Friend with Whom you could share your innermost secrets. What a comfort this should be, to know that you have one Friend Who fully knows you. There is no need ever to say again, "No one understands me!" Having been made like you, He is able to see both sides of where and what you are at all times. He sees the human side, for He once walked where you walk when He was on this earth to learn about you. He took upon Himself the fellowship of your sufferings that He might see through your eyes, hear through your ears, and touch with your senses the various experiences of life.

It is so common for others to pass judgment on you as they witness your failures and sins. Your mistakes seem so inexcusable, and others are always quite sure that *they* would never do what they watch *you* do. But Jesus never condemns you. He may not approve of your action, condone your sin, or excuse your failure; but He will never condemn you. He loves you, and fully understands and appreciates the pressures others cannot see that were at work in your heart; He sees and evaluates the fears, doubts, and conflicting emotions that drove you to your final conclusion. He will help you, chasten you, instruct and encourage you, but He will never condemn you; for it was this frustrated, confused and frightened little man He came to love and save.

You may feel free to talk openly about your feelings to Jesus. He is touched by the feelings caused by your weaknesses. Others criticize your weakness, but Jesus is concerned about your feelings. He knows what it is to be misunderstood, condemned without trial, criticized without others seeing both sides, and accused wrongly. When Simon Peter denied the Lord Jesus Christ, I am sure others, watching this failure by a man supposed to "know better," were quick to condemn and rebuke him. What moved the Lord Jesus when He looked at this bitterly weeping man was not his failure, but his feelings. Jesus knew ahead about Peter's weakness; but it was the honest tears that betrayed the deep hurt of his soul, that touched the very heart of the Saviour.

Jesus is the only friend you will ever have who can stand the full revelation of what you are. You need not ever hide from Him, nor wear a mask. He fully knows you, and you may walk with Him unashamed, though naked, in the full assurance that no revelation of yourself will ever dissipate His love and acceptance. If you are like Mephibosheth of old, and your feet are lame, you may uncover them in His presence and will only draw from His great heart the deepest kind of compassion and understanding. If you are at times as the bruised reed, He will never seek to break you. If the feeble flame of love and devotion becomes but a smoking lamp, He will never quench you. He will never ridicule, taunt, revile or humiliate you. He can only love you and assure you that it is *you* He loves, not your performance or dutiful works. Though for a season you may have been in the far country wasting your substance in riotous living, He will patiently wait until you have spent all, are in deep want, come to yourself and flee to His arms. He will show you nothing but His compassion, fall upon your neck and kiss your fears away. He will clothe you once more with Himself and rejoice in the reality of your renewed fellowship.

Like the Emmaus disciples, you may be going the wrong direction in life at this very moment, gloomy and sad, heart filled with unbelief and the future as black as midnight. He will overtake you as you walk, and patiently draw from your confused heart the details of your pent up feelings. He will abide with you when your day is far spent, break bread with your hungry heart, reveal Himself to you afresh and set your heart aflame with His undying love. Truly here is a Friend Who can tell you all things that ever you did, and Who knew you before you ever knew Him. Here is a friendship where communication will never break down; even when you get sullen and withdrawn, He will search you out and force you once more to the dialogue of love. He will pursue you, talk to you, make you listen and encourage you to pour out the contents of your heart in the assurance that He will fully understand. You need never explain to Jesus. The details are fully known to Him before you try. He will let you talk freely to Him if you wish; and when you do, your thoughts and feelings will take on a strange new perspective when you realize you are voicing them in the presence of One Who fully loves you.

Have you experienced the comfort of such a Friend? Will you not this very moment turn to Jesus in faith that He is with you and will never leave you, and pour out all that troubles and alarms you? Do not talk of being fit for His presence. He is your Friend! He will welcome you as you are. No wonder this hymn is one of the most beloved of all modern times:

"Just as I am, without one plea,
  But that Thy blood was shed for me,
And that Thou bidd'st me come to Thee,
  O Lamb of God, I come! I come!

"Just as I am, Thou wilt receive,
  Wilt welcome, pardon, cleanse, relieve;
Because Thy promise I believe,
  O Lamb of God, I come! I come!"

Dear reader, here at last is earth's one Friend of Whose company you will never tire. Though familiarity may breed contempt for all other persons, your growing familiarity with Jesus will only increase your love for Him and reveal more of the dimensions of His real love for you. It will take forever to unveil the many wonders of this wonderful One. Eternity will not tell all the meaning of the name written that He alone knows, and we call "Jesus." At last you may love Him with all your heart, and fully reveal yourself to Him without fear of ever losing His great love. That love has been eternally bestowed upon you, and it is yours to enjoy in life and death as an everlasting possession. It flows from God . . . fills your heart to overflowing . . . and spills out of you like a river of living water. No wonder Peter wrote, *"Unto you therefore which believe he is precious."*

I will ~~ever~~ be a friend who understands, but not condemns. He loves you as you are

THE FELLOWSHIP OF LOVE

Of all the shameful titles ascribed to our lovely Saviour, the most encouraging is this one: He was called a friend of sinners! Surely this description hurled in derision at Him must have pleased Him immensely, for He came to earth to be just that. Little did His enemies know that they had charged Him with the very thing that was dearest to His heart! No better place in His earthly life can this compassion and love of the Saviour for sinners be seen than in the lovely story related to us by the evangelist Luke in the 7th chapter of his Gospel, verses 33 to 50. Please read it for yourself and then let me retell this warm, moving experience for your encouragement.

Jesus had just concluded a stormy preaching session to the people, and some had believed His Word, but the Pharisees and lawyers had rejected the testimony of God against themselves. When it was over one of them, a man named Simon, insisted that Jesus go home with him to eat. (What grace Jesus demonstrated in accepting this invitation offered by His enemy!) While they sat at meat, a woman, unnamed, who was known in the city as a sinner (in the sense of unchaste), came in unannounced. Without a word she takes her place at the feet of Jesus, and to the shock of Simon, begins to weep openly; and as her tears splash upon the Saviour's feet, she kneels and with her long hair wipes them tenderly. Now, impulsively, she kisses His feet over and over in an overwhelming show of affection. Quickly now she takes an alabaster box of ointment she has brought with her, breaks it, and without a word anoints the feet that soon will be nailed to Calvary's cross for her.

When Simon recovered sufficiently from the initial shock of such disgusting conduct, he began to murmur within and accuse the Lord Jesus for allowing her to do what she did. His reasoning was that if Jesus were truly a prophet of God, He would have known what an unclean sinner woman she really was, since her reputation was known to all in the city; hence, had He really known who and what she was, He would never have allowed her to touch Him. Jesus, reading the innermost thoughts of Simon's heart, answered the charge with a parable.

A creditor had two debtors; one owed a small amount, the other a large amount. Neither one could pay, but the creditor frankly and freely forgave them both. Jesus then presses the point: *"Tell me therefore, which of them will love him most?"* Simon, obviously irritated, answers with sarcasm, "I *suppose that he, to whom he forgave most."* Jesus assures Simon he is correct in his judgment and quickly presses the point of the sword into Simon's heart as He explains: "Look at this woman, Simon; I came to your house and you never even offered me water for my feet, but she washed them with her tears. You never offered even to kiss me in greeting on my cheek, but since I arrived she has not ceased to kiss my feet. You did not anoint my head as is the custom due to all, but this dear woman anointed my feet with ointment. You see, Simon, this woman has had much forgiven her; and it has resulted in much love for me." I am sure Simon must have gotten the implication that he possessed no real love for Jesus because he had no realization of sins forgiven. I trust you will not forget this illustration; for it clearly shows that our love for Jesus, and His personal preciousness to us, is in exact proportion to our sense of sins forgiven.

But let me speak to you now about the dear woman's relationship with the one true Friend she had found in this life. Her reputation in the city may have been bad; her sins may have been known to all; but she had found in Jesus the forgiveness of all. The city couldn't forgive her; Simon wouldn't; but Jesus had freely and frankly forgiven her all. She believed and knew in her heart that in Jesus she had found the one man Who could fully accept and love her as she was. It was not the woman Simon saw and knew that Jesus loved, but the little woman inside of her that no man had ever seen but Jesus. She had found in Him the one man she could fully love with all her heart, and in Whose blessed presence she could be her real self without the fear of losing His love.

How real she is in His presence! She comes to Him just as she is, without pretence; without explanation of her actions and with no embarrassment; and by the impulse of her love, she expresses herself without fear of ridicule or rebuke. She is in the presence of her Friend, the one Who took the time to look beyond the reputation that shamed her and found the woman no one ever understood, nor wanted to.

Jesus loved this woman. Simon could not grasp that, but what Pharisee can? He loved her and forgave her freely, and then went to His death at Calvary to prove to her and Simon the reality of that love. His great love had begotten in her a deep love for Him. His love had called from her heart a self-sacrificial love for Him, for He had become the most precious person she had ever known. He was the only man she deemed worthy of her most precious possession, the alabaster box of ointment. She had given herself to many men, but none had ever been worthy of the priceless thing she had hidden away. Men had used her, and abused her; had spoken meaningless words of love to her; but in Jesus she had found a Friend Who was worthy of the gift she could give only once. That box was symbolic of the love of her heart. She did more than pour ointment that day—she poured *herself* upon the feet of Jesus. She gave to Him what no other person on earth could give Him—the unique, personal love of her heart for Himself.

She knew the cost He paid to love her; the loss of esteem He suffered in Simon's eyes told her. Jesus endured the reproach of men for her. His person and His ministry were questioned; He was under continual criticism, accused of ignorance about her; yet without a word to justify Himself, He loved her to the end. No amount of pressure by men, demons, or Satan could make Him disown her or deny the reality of His love and hers. His death at Calvary was the ultimate cost He paid. She brought Him shame and reproach; and for her sake, He was made of no reputation among men.

Apart from the personal joy He received in doing that which pleased His Father, loving her had also its eternal compensations. She needed Him. She never tried to use Him; she only loved Him. She never asked for anything, only longed to pour out on Him what she alone could give. She wept for the joy of her love for Him, washed His feet in gratitude with her tears, and wiped them with the symbol of her earthly glory—her hair. She kissed Him over and over, anointed Him and touched Him in real love. She warmed and refreshed Him, and made the trials of His life and death worthwhile. But if she needed the love and ministry He came to give her, it is equally true that He needed, and was pleased by, the love and ministry she alone could give to Him.

The Bible says that God, in order to satisfy the great love wherewith He loved us, sent Jesus Christ to die for us. In the eternal ages to come, God will reveal more and more of His grace and kindness to us as the workmanship of His love is seen in us. This unnamed, unworthy, unclean sinner woman will one day be displayed as the masterpiece of God's grace and love; the only poem He ever composed, and the ultimate expression of all He is. While Simon could only see and know the woman he took her to be, Jesus saw and knew the woman His love would create her to be; and His heart and eye were on an eternal "someday" when all creation would see the glory of His love revealed in her.

May you enjoy the perfect peace this dear woman knew in His presence, and may His love and friendship be as real to you as it was to her. When men condemn, criticize, and accuse you; when the reputation of your sins and failures hound and plague you; when no man cares for your soul; flee to the arms and presence of Jesus, and know—*you have a Friend!*

we need love of Christ, but God enjoys love from us as well.

THE DISCOVERY OF LOVE

Perhaps you are saying, "I *do* love Jesus and I know He loves me. I want to walk with Him this way and be honest and open with Him about myself. But what will happen when I fail? What will He think when I let Him down?" Remember, dear reader, you have never been loved as God loves you. All the love you have ever known has been a "performance" type of love that faded away when your performance became unacceptable. All your life, those who "loved" you expressed their disappointment in you when you failed to meet their expectations. It will be difficult for you to always rest in the perfect love of God that knows no disappointment in you.

You have also been the target of religious brainwashing that has taught you from childhood that God's love is no different from man's love. Religion has twisted, perverted and warped God's love into the likeness of man's love for so long that only the patience of the Holy Spirit can bring the little man inside of you to walk in complete rest and peace with Jesus. The traditions of man, taught for the commandments of God, have so blinded your mind that resting in the love of Jesus will be like testing the ice for strength. You will draw back in fear and shame as you see more of the man Christ died for; but I assure you that He will never draw back from you.

When iniquity abounds, it has a cooling effect

on the love of the saints. Like the Ephesians of old, we leave the warmth and reality of our first love with Christ as we get more and more concerned about our performance, and get our eyes off His perfect performance and love for us. Religion is so deceptive. Its purpose is to cover us with fig leaves and convince us that only as we present a lie as to our real selves can God continue to love us. It would teach us to walk by laws, rules, and regulations, so that we can continually score ourselves in our own eyes and others', rather than walk in openness and nakedness, and in the light with God, resting only on His perfect love at Calvary for us. Let me contrast the teaching of religion with the truth of God in this matter.

Let us suppose there is a book we shall call the book of your life. On the cover is your name, and on the first page, the date and place of your birth or earthly beginning. On the last page is the date of your death, or the coming of the Lord Jesus in the air for you, whichever occurs first. In between these two pages is a page for every day of your life. At some point in this book is the day of your salvation, or the day the Holy Spirit convicted you of your need of the Saviour and enabled you to believe God's record of His Son. On that day you passed from death to life by faith in the finished work of Jesus Christ at the cross for you. All the pages of your life preceding your salvation are black with sin. On the basis of these pages, God revealed your need of a Saviour.

Now it is exactly at this point in our illustration that the difference between religion with its deception, and the truth of God, comes into focus. Let me first show you religion's perspective. It teaches that all the pages past the day of salvation in your life are clean, white pages. Each day you are obligated to fill them in with works of righteousness in order to keep your fellowship with your heavenly Father "up to date."

Religion recognizes the possibility of failure, so you are taught that each night as you read the page of your life you must confess that which is sin, and by the miracle of erasure remove from those pages the awful blots of daily sins and failures. This requires diligent prayer and repentance on your part, and you cannot take your rest in any peace of heart until you are satisfied that the page now reads to the satisfaction of God. It is a clever way of putting on the fig leaves each night before we dare to walk with God in the cool of the day. It is Adam's practice of hearing His voice and hiding behind the trees of the garden in fear.

The long range effect of such practice is devastating. First, it encourages us to categorize sin, and separate our deeds, words and thoughts into large and small sins, and to conveniently forget those we don't want to remember or discuss in the presence of the Lord. Soon we imagine we are growing better and better, and that our flesh, which never changes until we are at last in the presence of the Lord, is growing more righteous by the day. Self-righteousness grows; we forget what manner of persons we really are, and fall into the shameful practice of condemning others to bolster our own self-righteous walk with God. The evidences of our sickness begin to appear as we talk only of sin as being "before I was saved" and say about others, "I could never do that!" We talk less about Jesus and more about our correct "doctrine." We babble on about "church" and our wonderful works, and testify loud and long to our unbroken fellowship with God. When we are called to "testify" about the preciousness of Christ, we are obliged to reach back into the dusty past to find some black "sin" before salvation to remember the pit from whence we were digged, and in order to conjure up some small amount of love and praise for the Saviour. As our consciousness of sin diminishes, the preciousness of and the fervent love for Jesus we once knew, diminishes in the exact proportion.

At this time it might be well for you to re-read the introduction to this book before continuing. In it I say that our precious doctrines work fine, and to our satisfaction, until some life circumstance appears that is unaffected by the desperate application of our "doctrine." What will you do when, reading over the day of your life, you discover the page filled with all the things you vowed you could *never* do; *would* never do; and anyone who *did* could not possibly be a Christian? What will you do in the day you find yourself denying the Lord with an oath, after so boldly proclaiming

74

Him as your Lord and Saviour? What will you do when you find yourself weeping bitterly over a day you cannot change? You will be driven to the conclusion that God never *did* love you, you never *were* a Christian, and Jesus never *was* your Friend; and as Job was advised, better to curse God and die.

Now let me tell you the truth as it is in Christ. The book of your life is not filled with black and white pages at all—*it is filled with all black ones!* Oh, how we need a new perspective of sin. The Bible declares that whatsoever is not of faith is sin. To keep the whole law, and yet offend in one small point, is to be guilty of the entire law! God says that sin, in its simplest definition, is to come short of the glory of God. The glory of God is His own blessed Son, Jesus Christ—and any thought, word or deed done this day that is short in any way of Jesus Christ in His perfection is sin in the sight of God. Any man who says he commits no sin as a Christian, lies, and the truth is not in him. Your whole book of life is one long, black record, and you should be thankful that God in His mercy and grace reveals only one page at a time for you to read. The pages, as far as He is concerned, are already filled in; for there is no time with Him. When He saw you and loved you, He saw all there was of you to see, from the very first page of your life until the very last.

Go back to the story of Gethsemane and see that as Jesus looked into the cup that night, He was reading the book of your life. He read *every* page to its bitter end. He saw, and learned for the first time, the *entire* sin of your life; and the shock of it nearly killed Him. Three times during the reading of your book, with sweat turning to blood in the torture of what He read, He stopped to beg His Father to spare Him the further horror of what He saw. He, Who never knew sin by experience, learned it in the pages of *your* book of life. Having finished it in one hour, He bowed to the love and will of God to save you from it all and bring you to His presence without spot. His submission in Gethsemane was simply, "Father, I have read the entire book. It is horrible. It is terrible—more terrible than I had ever supposed. But you love this person, and I love you; and if there is no other way to save that soul, then I will write *my name* in the place of *his,* and give account in your judgment for its contents." This is why we speak of a *substitutionary atonement.* He took your place, and gave you His very own in the Father's sight.

Jesus carried the book of your life to Calvary, and with His name in the place of yours, answered when God called you to judgment to collect the wages of your sin—eternal separation from Himself in outer darkness. When He cried, *"My God, my God, why hast thou forsaken me?"* He carried your book to hell and burned its pages in the fiery wrath of God. There He buried as deep as the deepest ocean, your sin and sins from the sight of God. When He was raised from among the dead ones to sit at the Father's right hand,

He came back without that book; and God promised never to remember your sins and iniquities against you. When the unsaved are made to stand before Christ in judgment, the books will be opened; but your book will *never* be opened, for Jesus opened it at Gethsemane, and accepted it at the cross as His; God read it and sent His Son to hell to destroy it forever.

You are the only one now reading the book. You are reading it one day at a time, for the whole revelation of that book and its contents in one day would kill you. It would destroy any possibility of faith enough to believe that God could ever love you and accept you as you really are. As the pages unfold, what you read will often stun, bewilder, shock and amaze you just as it did the Saviour in Gethsemane. They will frighten and alarm you, and you will, in your panic, grab at any fig leaf or tree you can find to hide from God and man. But dear reader, nothing on those pages will ever stun, bewilder, shock, amaze or disappoint Jesus, for He has already read them all and loves you in spite of what He knows about you. You are in the realm of time, but He is in the realm of eternity. Those black pages are not merely "under the blood" as religion teaches, but *carried away* as far as the East is removed from the West. As you read, you are not becoming a greater sinner than ever before; you are only discovering daily what a great sinner God knew you to be—so great that nothing less than the delivering up of His Son for you could save you from a certain hell.

You are not discovering new sins to be forgiven; you are seeing for the first time each day how many sins you have *already* been forgiven for Jesus' name's sake!

But, you say, does not the Bible teach that Christians are to daily confess their sins that they might be forgiven and cleansed? A careful meditation on John's first epistle will reveal to you that your fellowship with the Father is based on a joint participation in the eternal work of His Son Jesus Christ. Our sins *are* forgiven us for His name's sake. The confession John writes about is the continual attitude of the believer's heart toward sin and sins. The word "confess" means to agree with another, or to say the same thing as another. The believer's heart continually says the same thing as God's about his sin and sins — that Jesus Christ the righteous has once and for all satisfied (propitiated) God in our behalf. The cleansing is, according to John's own choice of words, a continuous, moment-by-moment cleansing by the precious blood of Christ. That eternal blood, now on the mercy seat in heaven, ever speaks to God of our once and for all forgiveness by the cross. To walk in darkness is to ignore this fact, and either say you have no sin and commit no sins, or to continually seek forgiveness for sins already forgiven you. Faithful to the covenant of Calvary sealed with the eternal blood of His Son, God walks with you in unbroken fellowship as you meet with Him at the mercy seat by faith. John did not write to give Christians a *license*

78

to sin, but to *comfort* them as they read the daily pages of their book of life; to ever lift their eyes from the page to look at their Advocate at God's right hand, and remember that sin and sins have already been dealt with. One look at the cross tells the man who has been there that God is right about his sin and sins, and blesses his heart with the assurance that he is forgiven and cleansed by a faithful God Who cannot lie.

Christians are not *sinless*, but *blameless* in the sight of a holy God by virtue of the perfect righteousness of Jesus Christ, His Son. It is not a question of what a Christian *can do;* it is a daily revelation of what he *has done,* and for which he has been fully forgiven in Christ.

Study the life of the man who first learned the truth of God's grace to sinners, the Apostle Paul. He described himself before he was saved as a blasphemer, and a persecutor, and injurious; but 35 years of walking with Jesus as he read the daily pages of the book of his life revealed to him that he was in reality the chief of *all* the sinners. Note that when he confessed this he did not say "I *was*," but "I *am* the chief of sinners." Years of daily discovery had revealed the growing proportion of his sinnerhood; and as his awareness of himself increased, so did his love for Jesus in the exact proportion. As time went on, the Christian life revealed to Paul that no good thing dwelt in himself except Christ, and being less than least of all the saints, he could only confess that whatever he was in the sight of God and man, he was by the grace of God.

If you think religion has not taken its toll among believers, then attend any prayer meeting when the saints testify about their relationship with Jesus. You will hear them searching the musty past (before they were saved) to recall some black deed to impress others with how much they had been forgiven. They sense no reality of sin or sins after salvation, and as they get farther away from the page of their salvation, the memory of sin *and* the Saviour fades proportionately.

I do believe that the entire Christian life is not for learning about Jesus as much as it is for learning about ourselves. We shall have all eternity to learn about God's grace and kindness to us in Christ, but only one lifetime to learn what we, the objects of that love and grace, really are. God's first question to man was *"Where art thou?"* and until we learn the answer, we shall know nothing of Who He is.

Simon the Pharisee knew much *about* God, but the woman with the alabaster box knew God *Himself* personally and intimately. Simon knew about *God,* but the sinner woman had learned much about *herself,* and that knowledge had revealed the loveliness of Jesus Christ to her heart. Many Christians pray like Paul, *"That I may know him . . . "* but forget that the preciousness of the Lord Jesus Christ in Paul's eyes was revealed at the dung pile where he saw himself as he really was. We spend so much of our time and prayer more concerned with the outer circumstances of our lives, ever wanting to analyze, change, adjust or alter them, while living almost in oblivion to the reality of what we are within. We see ourselves neither as great sinners nor successful saints—just removed from the reality of what we are and sensing no need of anything; hence the preciousness of the Saviour is no issue. How much better to know the crushing sense of sin and the heaviness of the sorrow it brings, than the nothingness of spiritual lethargy that deprives us of the reality of Jesus' love and presence!

Ask any Christian to speak to you of the preciousness of Christ, and his confession will be in direct proportion to his knowledge of himself. Paul points out in his Ephesian letter that eternity, composed of successive ages, or periods of time, will consist of progressive revelations of God's exceeding riches of grace and kindness to us through Jesus Christ. In the book of Revelation John sees the saints in heaven gathered around the throne singing to the Lamb of God,

"Thou art worthy . . . thou wast slain . . .
thou hast redeemed us to God by thy blood . . .
thou hast made us unto our God kings and
priests . . . . "

In order to enter into the wonder of all this eternal praise and worship, we must learn while in this life something of the true nature of the sinner He loved and saved. What value is the precious blood of the Lamb in all His glory, if you have not seen the vileness of the one for whom He died?

I do believe that our enjoyment and appreciation of heaven will be according to how much we have learned here of ourselves. Meditation upon this thought will reveal to you why most religious hymns are about a *place* instead of a *person.* No wonder most people are more concerned about the golden streets, the pearly gates and the river of life than they are about the sweet presence of the Saviour! It also explains the mystery of a strange statement by a dying saint in Germany many years ago. He was asked, as he stood with one foot in time and the other in eternity, "What do you consider the most precious thing you have learned while on this earth?" After some quiet reflection he answered, "Of all that I have learned, I am most grateful for the knowledge of sin; for had I not known what a sinner I am, I would never have known the preciousness of the Saviour." And so John the Baptist put it aptly when he said, *"He must increase, but I must decrease."*

Perhaps you are saying, "But I have so many unanswered questions!" Of course you do! If beauty is in the eye of the beholder, then listening must also be in the ear of him who listens. You can hear God's truth with the intellect, or with the ears of the heart. When Jesus was on the earth He so often said, *"Ye have heard it said . . . but I say unto you . . . "* They had been taught the precepts and traditions of man; but when they heard the Truth of God in the flesh "tell it like it was," they had the choice of gladly agreeing with the testimony of the Holy Spirit in their hearts, or arguing with their minds in order to protect their precious "doctrine" and righteousness. This very fact is what stirred up so much resentment among the Jews against Him. He was not preaching some new thing, but only preaching in truth what they themselves professed to believe. Jesus practiced what the Pharisees taught; and they hated Him for it!

All fundamental, evangelical Bible believers teach salvation by grace alone based on the merits of Jesus Christ. Is it not strange how those who preach and teach salvation by grace, without merit on the sinner's part, manifest so little of the reality of it? I am encouraging you to walk in the reality of what they teach; and I do not expect to be treated any differently than my Saviour was. It is a choice between the righteousness of God in Christ alone, or self-righteousness and acceptance based on our continued performance and works.

If your deeds are evil and you seek only an excuse to sin more, then you will hear in this message a license for your sin. If fatalism appeals to you as an excuse for your ungodliness, then your ears will hear in this message an approval of your "what will be, will be" philosophy. If you have no desire to perform for the glory of God, then you will welcome this message as a blessed relief from duty. If the intent of your heart is only to "use" Jesus for your own ends and self glory, then you will work out your own perversion of this truth to satisfy your wicked heart.

On the other hand, if you are truly born of God and have longed for some word from Him that will take away your fears, relieve your doubts, and restore the joy and security of your walk with Him when sin and sins raise their vile head, then you will welcome the truth you read. If you learn that you never have to perform in order to continue in His love, then you will have an awakened desire to perform as never before to please Him Who can do nothing but love you. If you have been weakened, humbled and shaken by the reality of sin as you read the daily pages of your life, then you will be driven by these words to the rest, peace and shelter in Jesus Christ.

When the woman taken in the very act of adultery was brought by the Pharisees to Jesus to be stoned, He refused to hear her accusers. He paid no attention to their condemnation, but saw only the woman. When He looked at her He did not see the law, for it would be nailed to the cross in His own body and He would bear its curse for her. He did not see her sin, for it too would be fastened there under the wrath of God in His own dear body. He saw her only through the eyes of His Father Who loved her from before the foundation of the world. He had but one word for her heart: *"Go, and sin no more."* As she went away clothed in the mantle of such unearthly love she must have said to herself, "Jesus loves me and understands me, though He knows my sin. Oh, that I might sin no more and learn to love Him as He loved me!" Paul said the love of Christ

84

constrained him; the silken bands of real love constrain, when the law with all its threats cannot. This kind of love fulfills the entire law and can only beget a response of love that empties out our lives for His glory.

To lay hold of grace and love as it really is, is to make life worthwhile. It will enable you to face tomorrow with boldness, knowing that no new evidence will ever be introduced into your relationship with God that was not presented at Calvary and silenced forever. You can face each day without fear, knowing that when it is over you will love Jesus more than yesterday, but less than tomorrow. Each page of life with its failures and sins will only humble you, increase your need for Jesus, and make Him more precious than ever before. Judas hung himself in remorse, for he had never known the Saviour's love; but Peter wept bitterly over the same sin, for he could not deny that in spite of all he had discovered about himself, Jesus still loved him and he loved Jesus!

Discovery of love will make us love & appreciate ① more and more as times goes by b/c He has already ~~through~~ born our sins, ~~that we haven't~~ Even the sins we ~~are~~ will commit.

THE PATIENCE OF LOVE

After all, the acid test of any teaching is to take it to the laboratory of life and apply it to the reality of our experiences. The wounds of Jesus never took on any significance to Thomas until he looked at them in the glaring light of his own bitter unbelief. One look at the Saviour who was willing to be further hurt by Thomas in order to remove his doubts, caused him to see the wretchedness of his own wicked heart and to cry: *"My Lord and my God!"* Let us look at one day in the life of Simon Peter and put these truths to the test.

No other character in the New Testament is so completely or strangely sketched as is Simon Peter. A paradox of contradictions, he is the portrait of every believer in Christ. He was impulsive, harsh, cold of heart, slow to see the truth, cowardly, self-seeking, weak, insecure, inconsistent to his beliefs, forward, rash, and certainly talky. At the same time he was tender, affectionate, deep in the truth, courageous, self-sacrificial, immovable as a rock, bold, loving, forthright, humble, meek, and beautiful, for Jesus made him so. Self-assured and often arrogant, he was the spokesman for the apostles and made his boast about his undying devotion and love for Jesus Christ. His intentions were good, and he meant to keep his vows. He intended to prove the sincerity of his promises, and meant to die with or for Jesus. But there was one thing Peter must learn: he must learn the deceitfulness and desperately wicked nature of his own heart.

Peter had an awful lot of religion he didn't know he possessed. When Jesus predicted that His friends would deny Him, Peter firmly avowed that though *others* might, certainly not *he!* He added that he was ready to do or die as the situation demanded. Like most Christians, Peter had a preconceived idea of the Christian life. He was sure of what a Christian *could* or *could not* do, and was also quite sure that all others had the capacity to *do* what he was certain he could *never do*. Positive that he could handle any situation and that Satan had no tricks he could not evade, he walked in self-confidence, self-righteousness and pride. But pride goes before a fall, and a fall was in the future for this man.

It was like a programmed thing in his life. Jesus warned him ahead of time, and spoke of Peter's coming denial of Him as though it were already history. Satan had asked permission of the Lord to sift Peter like wheat, and Jesus had given him that permission. There was a valuable purpose in it all. Peter will learn about *himself;* be made real, compassionate, honest, humble, and usable. He will find a new rest in Jesus as he finds out what kind of man he really is, and by the love of Jesus will become a usable vessel in His hands. Satan will learn that though Peter failed, Jesus did not fail; and that the faith that was in Peter's heart was not *his* at all, but the faith of *God* that would never quit, no matter what the test.

Jesus knew ahead of Peter's failure; and the very feet that would stand with His enemies, Jesus bowed to wash in the upper room a few hours earlier. Jesus prayed for him, and promised that his faith would not fail and that he would be converted to strengthen his brethren—a better man in spite of his sin. See the thing unfold as Peter follows Jesus afar off to the judgment hall, sits with Jesus' enemies, warms himself at their fire, and to his own amazement hears himself deny the Lord he loved. Not *once,* but *thrice,* and with an oath!—not profanity as some suppose, but worse—calling on God in heaven to send upon him the severest penalty if he were found to lie in his denial. So deep was his sin that he called on the Father of our Lord Jesus Christ to aid him in his wickedness! Oh, how much Peter learned that night about himself, and how much more he was to learn about his precious Saviour!

The midnight hour has finally come for this proud, arrogant man. The moment he vowed would *never* come; the deed he said *others* might do, but not *he*; the fall he had expected of all, *has become his!* Here is the crushing of a man . . . spiritual suicide in the eyes of men. He will never be the same again, he thinks; broken, humbled, and humiliated, he raises his eyes only to meet the gaze of Jesus. Now see Peter, and hear him as his breast heaves, rising and falling with each successive sob. His voice rises to a pitch as he wails openly and weeps bitterly over his failure that day. He is filled with the overwhelming conviction that Jesus will forsake him forever, and the shame of what he really is becomes more than he can bear. All the pent up self-confidence, pride, courage and self-sufficiency spill out in his tears like a flood. For a moment his vision is filled with only his sin and failure, and he has in the heat and passion of this moment, forgotten the love and faithful promise of the Saviour to restore him in newness of faith and use him for His glory.

I often think of his innermost thoughts that night. I wonder if he said, *"I,* His companion and confessor, the man who stood with Him and declared Him to be the Christ, the Son of the living God; *I* who once walked on the water, preached His gospel, was healed by His power, left all to follow Him, vowed never to do the thing I have now done—*I have denied the only Friend I ever had!"* How could he have done this thing? But, more important, how will he ever *live* with it? He cannot rest in the bold confession he once made, for his present denial has made it of no effect. He cannot rest in promises of future performance, for he can never again vow what he *will* or *will not* do—this moment has revealed the folly of such promises. He cannot be encouraged or comforted by the brethren, for they can never believe in him again. How can they excuse a man who had so much light, who accompanied Jesus to Gethsemane and heard Him pray? If a man is more blessed in believing without seeing, surely he is more condemned in denying after having seen!

To add to his shame, while he is yet weeping he remembers the words of the Lord. Jesus had warned him and prepared him for this very moment. When Peter walked on the water and began to sink it was Jesus Who caught him, and now it must be Jesus alone Who will catch him again. When others forsook the Lord it was Peter who answered Jesus' question, *"Will ye also go away?"* with *"To whom shall we go?"* Now there is no one to turn to but Jesus. At the transfiguration when he was on his face, afraid, it was Jesus Who touched him and lifted him up to see no man but Jesus only. Now, Jesus must lift him up again. In the upper room it was Peter who said Jesus should never wash his feet; now, if Jesus does not wash his feet he will be unclean forever. He slips out into the night for three days of soul searching and sorrow, and he is strangely absent at the cross.

> *"And men took note of his gloomy air,*
> *The shame in his eye, the halt in his prayer,*
> *The signs of a battle lost within,*
> *The pain of a soul in the coils of sin.*
>
> *"Into the desert alone rode he,*
> *Alone with the Infinite Purity;*
> *And bowing his soul to its tender rebuke,*
> *As Peter did at the Master's look,*
> *He measured his path with prayer and pain,*
> *For peace with God and nature again."*
> *(Whittier)*

90

But another scene is unfolded in this man's life . . . a happier day. It is three days and nights later, and Peter is at the tomb to learn the joy of Jesus' resurrection, and meets with the disciples that night around His blessed person. There is not a mention of his sin—not a rebuke, nor a word of condemnation! A few days later this same broken, humbled man stands once more as the spokesman of those who believed, and in the power of the Holy Spirit he preaches Christ to the nation. How can Peter have such boldness in the face of such recent failure? How *dare* he speak the name of Jesus again after such a recent denial? How can he look men in the eye again after sinning against such light?

The answer is revealed in the Bible. We are told that the Lord Jesus appeared privately to Peter after the resurrection. In that face to face encounter, shrouded in secrecy, the boldness, joy and peace of Peter's heart was restored, and once more he walked with Jesus in the reality of His fellowship. I can only guess at what went on in that meeting. There, in the wounds of the Saviour's hands and side, Peter saw that though *his* performance had failed, *Jesus* had faithfully performed in his behalf. Peter was not restored, but *reassured* that Jesus' love for him had never changed. Had He not foretold the very thing Peter would do? Had He not known ahead about his denial? Had He not promised to pray, and assured him that his faith would not fail? Though the shameful thing had stunned, shocked and bewildered Peter, it had not disappointed, discouraged, or dissipated the Saviour's love for him. Perfect love had cast out Peter's fear. The preciousness of Jesus' love appeared as never before in the glaring light of his little love. Peter's religion, courage, determination, promise, performance, reputation and image had failed in his eyes and others'; but *Jesus' love had not failed,* for in spite of all Peter saw in himself, he could not deny that he sincerely loved the Saviour and that the Saviour loved him.

Say what you will about the denial Peter made that night, but apart from it could Peter ever have learned that Jesus loved the little man inside? Would he not have always thought that Jesus loved the strong image man who performed satisfactorily, and who confessed and defended the Lord so vigorously? There at the secret meeting between Jesus and Peter, he learned that the love Jesus had bestowed upon him was never earned, deserved, or fully appreciated. At the judgment hall, Peter showed himself for what he really was; and yet the Saviour sought him, needed him, and loved him with *real* love.

The secret of his boldness at Pentecost was this: *"Jesus loves me, this I know."* There was no need to justify himself in any man's eyes! No need to explain his act, for no man could understand— only Jesus. No need to worry over the loss of friends; Jesus was his friend! That black night was between himself and Jesus, and the cross of Calvary anticipated it all. Knowing that God in Christ had accepted him as he was, enabled Peter to accept himself as he was and made him a usable vessel from that day on. Oh, <u>what a strength he must have been to discouraged, failing, sinning brothers!</u> Peter knew what it was to be broken, afraid, heartsick and discouraged. As a shepherd among the sheep of Jesus, this man had known the weakness of the weakest sheep and the strength of the strongest. Having seen himself as he really was, his heart had been made tender to the needs of his brothers, and their feelings would move him to the deepest compassion. Resting in his acceptance by God <u>through the sacrificial death of Christ; walking in glad fellowship with Jesus, naked and unashamed; his guilt and insecurity wiped away by the love and grace of Calvary, Peter was now ready to accept others as they were.</u>

It's not that we were sinners & now we're perfect. We were sinners & cont. to be sinners. It is the love of Christ that sustains us @ the point of Justification, and it is the love of Christ that Sustains us @ thru out glorification. Looking @ Peter, he had his limits & he was a sinner, but ① continued to love & trust Him and that allowed Peter to live w/o insecurity & t. love others as ① loved. (as they are)."

THE LIBERTY OF LOVE

Once you have discovered the real love of God in Christ, you will become more and more aware of the liberty there is in Him. To know Him aright is to experience life abundant, and no other place will this be so apparent as in your relationship with others. Walking with Jesus in unbroken fellowship; assured of His undying love and acceptance with God your Father; and freed of your guilt, sense of inadequacy and fears, you will, for the first time in your life, be free to be loved and to love others. True and real love will be at home and at work in you, and some of life's greatest moments await you. Loneliness will be ended as the impulsive love of Christ reaches through you to others in their need.

Before returning to heaven via the cross, the Lord Jesus gave a new commandment:

"This is my commandment, That ye love one another, as I have loved you."

A more literal translation might read: *"All my teachings are to the end that you should love one another."* The daily experience of this miracle of loving others as He loved you will also be the daily assurance of your real relationship with Him. Those who truly love Him in the reality of saving faith, keep this commandment. The love that you have for Him will burst forth in real love for others. Loving your brothers is evidence of dwelling in the light and is proof that you really do know Him.

When God's love in Christ dwells in you, you will find that you cannot shut up the door of your heart to others in need, for once knowing *how* He loved you, you cannot *help* loving others.

The keeping of this commandment is not grievous, for His callings are His enablements. He is your Lord; and His very command for you to love others as He loved you, assures your heart of the certainty of its fulfilment. His love will constrain you, for He loved you in order that you might experience His love for others through you. No man can love another with real love until he first of all has learned *how* to love, by *being* loved of God through Jesus Christ. No one can write a "how-to-do-it" book on loving others. No rules, procedures, regulations, limitations or logic can be applied to the free love of Christ through those who know Him. Knowing the manner of His love for you is all you need to know about loving others. The Holy Spirit will teach you *whom* to love, and *how* to love, and will work the mystery of the fellowship of love in your heart as you learn from Him.

We are taught of God how to love, for love is the fruit of the Holy Spirit in us as we yield to Him. Did He not teach you to pray by groaning in you with sighs that baffle words? Did He not teach you that you cannot speak forth the mysteries of the gospel to others without His opening a door of utterance for you? Is it not true that there are some with whom we enjoy the unspeakable privilege of telling the story of Jesus and, just as true, there are others in whose presence we stand mute? It is not always our *unwillingness* to be used of the Spirit of God. The mystery of His enablement lies at times in the sovereignty of Himself. When Philip stood by the desert highway, many chariots must have gone by until the Spirit said, *"Go near, and join thyself to this chariot."* There were many prisoners in the Philippian jail, but it was the jailer to whom the Spirit enabled Paul to say,

"Believe on the Lord Jesus Christ, and thou shalt be saved."

There were many women in Samaria when Jesus rested at the well of Jacob, but it was that one woman about whom He knew all things, that He went out of His way to reach. There were many rulers among the Jews, but it was Nicodemus who was strangely drawn to Jesus by night to learn the way of life. As you walk in the Spirit, you will marvel at the unexpected times and persons upon whom He is pleased to bestow the love of Christ. Jesus said by this means all men would know that you are His disciple. A disciple is a learner, and you will learn daily of the limitless dimensions of His love, and enjoy the blessed privilege of watching Him love others through you.

The love that flows among the saints is not as religion teaches — a painful duty, a dreary obligation, and a wearisome task. We do not grit our teeth, tolerate those we do not like, and say "I love you" simply to prove that we love the Lord. That may be *religious* love, but it is not *Christian* love! It is very obvious that if the work of *real love* through the saints is the work of the Holy Spirit bearing the fruit of the Lord Jesus Christ within, then *religious love* is the work of false spirits abroad in the world. All of us have seen much of it. Many of us have found that the "love" so freely offered once, was suddenly withdrawn when we no longer attended the church that "loved" us. Some of us have seen that the so-called "love" once bestowed on us was just as quickly revoked when our performance did not match the expectations of those that "loved" us. Religious love has no capacity to love an erring brother, finds no desire to place upon him a mantle of love that will cover the multitude of his sins, and has no patience to endure him long enough to restore him. Religion offers mere *performance* love masquerading under the guise of *Christian* love, and it is a mockery to the real love experienced by true believers. Religious love loves only the righteous (in their eyes), the acceptable (according to their standards), the good (measured by themselves), and the lovely (those reflecting their own likeness), but disappears like spring snow in a warm sun when the object of their affections provides no cause for their love.

In order to hide the true nature of this counterfeit that religion offers to others as "Christian" love, they often try to explain the difficulties of it by saying, "When we can find no cause to love others, then we are to love them because Christic

is in them. It is really Jesus in them that we love."
This is just the opposite of Jesus' love for you! To
say we are to love another because Christ is in
him is a clever but cruel way of brushing aside the
man himself in one fell swoop. It is a sure way of
sending the little man inside of him scurrying
back to his lonely prison, more sure than ever that
no one can *really* love him as he is, but only *tolerate*
him for Christ's sake. Jesus said we would love
one another as He loved us; the *man* would be
loved, not Jesus in him. How did He love you?
When you were without strength, unlovely, a
sinner, defiled, ruined, and His enemy! Not when
you performed satisfactorily, but when your performance sent Him to hell. Not when you pro-
vided Him with pleasure, but when you brought
Him pain. Not as you delighted His heart, but
when you were a reproach that delivered Him to
His death. Such is the manner of His love for you,
and His promise is that you will love others in
the same manner. Not to the same *degree,* or ex-
tent, for that would be impossible for any of us;
but on the same *grounds*—freely and without
cause in the beloved. We do not love others because Christ is in *them,* but rather because Christ
is in *us!* This glorifies *His* love for you and them,
not *your* love for Him.

Again, I remind you that real love flows from
God the source, and must flow outward from Him
without merit in the unworthy. In your experience
with others you will find that it does just this;
oftentimes to your great surprise and amazement,

you will discover Jesus Himself loving the un-lovely through you. John the Apostle agrees with this principle, for he wrote,

> "Herein is love, not that we loved God, but that he loved us . . . . "

God did not love you because Jesus was in you. Quite the contrary! God loved you when there was no good thing at all in you. He loved you just as you were and accepted you in the full merits of another, His blessed Son, and loved you with the love wherewith He had loved the Son since before the foundation of the world. I am so glad that the real love I have enjoyed from my brethren has not been because they saw Jesus in me, for they have seen so little of Him and so much of what I really am. I can walk naked and openly with them in that love, for I know that they will never discover anything in me that will discourage or destroy the love they give. It is not them loving me because Christ is in me; it is Jesus loving *me,* this I know, because *He is in them!*

As you learn more about yourself, and con-sequently more about the real nature of Jesus' love for you, you will find that there is no more logic in your love for others than there is in His love for you. Oh, dear reader, as Jesus reaches out to love others through you, do not resist Him! His love through you will be impulsive and un-predictable and often terrifying. It will terrify you because you will sense the absolutely un-controllable nature of it. It will burst forth at the most unexpected times and flood out of your heart

99

to fill the most unlikely persons, like a river of living water. It will break down every barrier man has erected to keep "love" in its proper channels, and will bring the rebuke of the world around you for the reckless direction of your love. Jesus' love will break all the rules of others, sweep over every line of demarcation, embrace the unlovely; and will, like lightning, strike where it pleases. Do not try to analyze, scrutinize, approve or hinder it; just let Jesus love through you whomsoever He desires to love in order that He might show the manner in which His Father loved Him and you. His love is in His own control, not yours, and you are the blessed vessel through which He has been pleased to love others.

Like Jesus, who loved the rich young ruler at first sight, you may, upon beholding another, feel the surge of Jesus' love through you for that person, though he is unknown to you. He is known and loved of Jesus, and you are the instrument through which He intends to reach and love that person. He loved you because it was His nature to love and He could not help Himself; and you will find yourself loving others because you cannot help yourself. Follow your heart as His love constrains you, and do not say that God is in your heart, but rather say that you are in the heart of God.

THE PURPOSE OF LOVE

The Father loved the Son in the beginning, and longed that all His creation would know the majesty of His love; this glorifies Him, for He *is*—LOVE. He sent the Son to earth to reveal His name to you that you might know and love Him. The Lord Jesus Christ went to Calvary to prove the reality of the Father's love for Himself and for you. Now, Jesus Christ dwelling in you sends you forth, as He was sent of the Father, to demonstrate the reality of this love to others. As the Father does not *work* at loving the Son, and the Son does not *work* at loving the Father, so you will not have to *work* at loving others. As you walk with Him He will search out others He desires to reach and love for Himself, and you will share the joy and pleasure of this blessed experience. Real love must contact others in some perceptible way. Jesus' love for others must be realized through some personal touch with reality; for if anyone is to know that Jesus loves them, someone must bring Jesus and His love to them in life. You are *where* you are, that Jesus might be *there*. He will walk the dusty roads of life as He did the Emmaus road, disguised through you as a stranger, to overtake those who are discouraged, afraid and miserable. He will talk with them through you, become their friend, break bread with them and reveal Himself through your heart, that their hearts might be set ablaze with love for

Himself. Their eyes will be opened and they will see that it was *Jesus* loving them all the time, not *you*.

As He sent Titus to the Apostle Paul to love, encourage and comfort him, He will send you to others that He might help them to "make it through the night" by knowing His love and friendship. You will be His love-gift to them, and they will be enabled to receive the love bestowed upon them. So many people are yet hiding behind the trees of the garden, afraid of God and man, certain that no one loves or cares for their soul; guilty and ashamed of what they see themselves to be; wearing a mask and playing their roles reconciled to a life of loneliness without love. Jesus loves them and longs to search them out through you, and bring them out of their prison into the life and liberty of His presence and love. We cannot carry only the *theology* of love to those who perish in their loneliness, and expect them to be impressed. We must also *touch* their hearts with Jesus' love and demonstrate in deed, as God did for us, the reality of this eternal love. Someone in whom Jesus dwells must come *where* they are and love them with real love *as* they are; become their friend to whom they can reveal themselves fully without fear or shame, that they might learn that it is *Jesus* Who has found them, *Jesus* Who knows them, and *Jesus* Who loves them.

Oh, what joy will be yours as you watch the little man inside of others brought to life by the love of Jesus!—like a rosebud at first, hard, closed up to all, their real face and loveliness hidden from God and man—until the warmth and life of the love of Christ begins to reveal the loveliness He creates and only He could see. They were precious in His sight, and their loveliness was in the eye of the One Who beheld them.

"I think true love is never blind, but rather brings an added light, an inner vision quick to find the beauties hid from common sight."

As His joy is fulfilled in you, your heart will comprehend the simplicity of His Word, *"It is more blessed to give than to receive."* Greater than being loved is the ability *to love* another, and watching Jesus love others through you is life's greatest blessing.

When you were saved, or fell in love with Jesus because He first loved you, many wonderful things happened to you. Among them, you were joined to the mystical body of Christ. The scriptures picture the true church, or assembly of saints, whose names are written in heaven, as a body over which Christ is the Head. He is seated in heaven at the right hand of God's throne, and also present in the church on earth by His Holy Spirit. The moment you were saved, the Holy Spirit placed you in living union with that body, and made you to share the common life of that body which flows from its Head. Like a real physical body, the body of Christ has many members but all do not have the same function or ministry. All contribute to the welfare of the body, but not all members perform the same way. Each supplies what it can to the parts of the body dependent upon it, and all grace and supply flows from the Head. Your place in that body is according to His pleasure, and is for the purpose of allowing Jesus to do through you what needs to be done for the welfare of the body in general, and the good of its members individually.

Of all the gifts that are ministered by Jesus to the body, the most excellent of all is love. Every member of the body needs love—*real* love—*Jesus'* love ministered to them through others. Some members, so the scripture teaches, need more than others. These members are called feeble, less honourable, uncomely, and those parts which lack. Jesus is concerned over their state, and exercises great care in loving them in more abundant ways according to their needs. Deep calleth unto deep, and the deep love needs of each individual member are answered by a deep supply of love by Jesus through others. As water seeks its own level, it is also true that those who want and need to experience more of the love of Christ, will have a more abundant supply. As they reach out to Him in their need, He reaches back to them to meet them in their desire. Each member is given grace according to the measure of the gift of Christ. This is in order to bring that member to maturity in the love of Christ, to enable him to minister in his place, and to edify the entire body in love. Each of us has something of love to supply to the body; and through the Head, nourishment is ministered to every part in order to knit the whole body together and to cause it to increase with the increase of God.

With this understanding, you will find Jesus loving some through you with what seems to be a *greater* degree of love than others. Some have a greater capacity to *receive*, and some have a greater capacity and need to *give* love. Each finds his needs met in the body as Jesus regulates and controls that love through the members. Each of us also enjoys a personal manifestation of Jesus to share with others in the body. We are unique personalities with varied abilities to reflect the love of Christ in proportion to His personal preciousness to us. The more you reach out to Him, the greater appreciation of His love you have, and hence, a unique revelation of Himself to share with others.

Do not be concerned when you are criticized for loving one more abundantly than another, for I truly believe that no degrees of love exist, only differences in the manifestation of that love. Some *seem* to love Jesus more than others, but it is only because of a deeper appreciation of how much they have been forgiven. Jesus is pleased with the *little* or *much* of our love, and desires only that we increase in love more and more. The same holds true with our love for others. Each member of the body will call out of your heart a special manifestation of Jesus' love for that person that no other can call forth. As I have already illustrated, it is so with our children. I cannot say that I love one of my children more

105

than another. If one of my children were to die, I could not take the love I have for that child and bestow it upon another. It was called out of my heart by the unique personality of that child and cannot be transferred to another. Do not, therefore, try to love all the same, but allow Jesus to love each individual in the manner He chooses through you. Let the liberty of love be your daily joy, and always remember that Jesus Christ alone is the Lord of love. Let Him love through you whomsoever He pleases, in whatever manifestation He enables you to give. Love is not something you can *do.* It is He alone Who can love others as He has loved you, and He will direct the course and intensity of that love as you yield to Him for His glory.

As your love for others becomes a reality in your life, do not be discouraged by the troublesome rules and regulations of the religious world around you. Real love stirs up the wrath of religion, for their own lack of it is brought into the glaring light of public discovery. They will tell you that if you cannot love *all* alike, then it is wrong to love *any.* I have observed over the years this false notion forced upon believers as a cover-up for the obvious lack of real love for *any.* Loud and long are the earnest appeals they give to love the whole world, while at the same time never manifesting any real love at all for the individual nearest to them. They weep public tears for the "unevangelized" while the man who sits across the desk from them day after day perishes for love, and they never even know he is alive. Do not be concerned if you cannot love *many*—be thankful if you can love *any* with a love that is real and is the result of Jesus loving through you. Never apologize for not loving some, and never apologize for Jesus loving others by you. Never hinder another from the sovereign display of Jesus' love through them, and never allow others to hinder His love from flowing through you in whatever direction He pleases. If your life is spent in loving just *one* as Jesus loved you, it will be a life well spent, and will show to all men around you that you have learned the secret of love from Jesus. After all, Jesus left heaven for *you*; and had you been the only soul on earth, He would have come from the glory, lived in shame, died in rejection for your sins, descended into hell, ascended into heaven and presented His blood to God *just for you!*

Always remember that you live in a world that ever seeks to bring you into the slavery of ideas, notions, rules and traditions that would regulate, control, and dispense love only to those it deems worthy. You live in a world that equates "love" with "sex", and all display of love outside the home is judged "improper", "wrong," and "illegal." You will always be the target of unloving people who, enraged by the honesty of Jesus' love in you, will condemn and accuse you. Jesus was hated and ultimately crucified for daring to love the unlovely, walk with the sinner, and be the Friend of the friendless. If the world heard

Him, they will hear you. If they hated Him without a cause, they will hate you also. Rejoice! Your
name is written in heaven, and the fellowship of
His sufferings only assures you of the reality of
His life within.

As Jesus loves others through you, the cost
of love will become more apparent—not merely
the criticism of the unloving, but the self-sacrifice
that is called from your heart.

*"Greater love hath no man than this, that a
man lay down his life for his friends,"*

Jesus said. In His case it meant His actual life
laid down as the Good Shepherd at Calvary. For
Paul it had a different meaning; he poured out his
life as a drink offering upon the sacrifice and
service of the faith of the Philippians. As you see
the need of those Jesus loves through you, your
heart will be opened, and the bowels of your
compassion will move you to give of yourself in
love to them. Someone said that rings and brace-
lets are not gifts, but *excuses* for gifts. The only
real gift of love any of us can give is *ourselves.*
Those we love need a friend—someone to whom
they can reveal their real selves and their innermost thoughts; someone to whom they can tell
their deepest fears without shame, and their
fondest dreams without ridicule; another self,
to whom they can utterly trust themselves as they
are, without the fear of losing the love they enjoy.
To bring another to the safety and security of
Jesus' love requires that we give ourselves in the
same honesty—take off our fig leaves and walk

in the boldness of love with them. We cannot wear a mask and ask others to remove theirs. We cannot offer an image and expect others to be real with us. Many a lonely soul sits deep within his prison watching the faces of all who pass his way for one who will take the time to look behind his mask to find and love the little man inside.

It is recorded in the Bible that John was the disciple Jesus loved. Four times this statement is made about this man. Have you ever wondered what there was about John that caused the Holy Spirit to record for all time the fact of Jesus' special love for Him? Peter was the spokesman for the disciples, the preacher and leader. He confessed Him before all, and it was he who drew his sword to defend the Lord in Gethsemane. But John is the *beloved* of Jesus. No special ministry or accomplishments are ascribed to John, yet he is singled out to lie on the bosom of the Lord at the last supper, to have his personal questions answered directly by the Lord Jesus, and to be designated four separate times as the special object of His affections.

Perhaps the secret of this mystery is in the teaching of the Saviour when He said that His friends would be those through whom He would love others as He had loved them. John was known as the apostle of love, and wrote more on the subject than any writer of the Bible. Perhaps John was a special friend through whom Jesus had manifested His great love to others; if this is true, then we need search no further for the meaning behind the words, *"the disciple whom Jesus loved."* No wonder Jesus committed to John at the cross the care of the dearest person on earth to Him—His mother. My prayer for you is that you shall have a fervent desire to be a special friend to Jesus by yielding your heart and life to Him as a channel for His great love to others. He is *your* Friend—may your heart's desire be to be *His* friend!

My desire for you to be Jesus' special friend is also the desire of my own heart, and my continual prayer. Often during the writing of this book I have stopped to beseech my Father to love through me as He has loved me. When that moment of my life comes that I am called to the presence of the Lord Jesus, I pray that I may be remembered on earth as the friend of Jesus. If I could enjoy but one reputation above all, I would covet John's, for it was a more excellent way. I would rather be known as a disciple of love than to be called the "prince of preachers." Though I could speak in all the languages of men; be eloquent as an angel; prophesy with deep insight; understand and explain the mysteries of God; if I could demonstrate faith that moves mountains to the wonder of those around me, or be known for my generosity in bestowing all my goods to feed the poor, or die a martyr's death to show my devotion to God—yet if all these marvels did not issue from the reality of the love of Christ in me, I would still be a useless nobody. My desire is simply to know that Jesus loves me, and that others will know that He has found one through whom He may love others as He loves me!

Once a number of moths were circling a candle. One of them inquired, "What is that strange object?" After much discussion they agreed that the way to know was for one of them to investigate more closely. A volunteer flew closer to the candle than any had dared before. Upon returning he reported that he had discovered the candle to be a great light. In that light he had seen things never seen before, and his enthusiasm for the light he had found caused them all to desire that light. But one moth was not satisfied that this was all there was to know about the candle, so against the warning of his friends, he flew still closer to the light. When he returned he proclaimed with great joy that he had found more than light; it was also heat, and it had warmed him in the chilly darkness. Another moth longed to fly closer than that, and with reckless abandon bade his friends good-bye, and flew into the light to be consumed by the intensity of its flame.

We are so much like those moths. Some of us are content to know the Lord Jesus Christ only as light for our path and a lamp unto our feet. Others, pressing closer to Him than ever before, have discovered the warmth of His friendship, and their own hearts are made to burn within by the reality of His fellowship. May you and I, dear reader, have a deep desire to lie on the bosom of our Lord until the intensity of His great love consumes us, and we are found no more. May His love fill us until others see no man, save Jesus only.

"Oh, the bitter pain and sorrow
  That a time could ever be
When I proudly said to Jesus—
  'All of self and none of Thee.'

"Yet He found me; I beheld Him
  Bleeding on the accursed tree;
And my wistful heart said faintly,
  'Some of self and some of Thee.'

"Day by day His tender mercy,
  Healing, helping, full and free,
Brought me lower, while I whispered—
  'Less of self, and more of Thee.'

"Higher than the highest heavens,
  Deeper than the deepest sea,
Lord, Thy love at last has conquered:
  'None of self and ALL of Thee.' "

THE POTENTIAL OF LOVE

The present lovelessness of professing Christianity seems to satisfy most today, yet one cannot read the history of the early church without being impressed with the contrast of the then and now. Christianity was born in a society much like ours today. It was a time when philosophy and reason reigned, and all the religions of the Greeks and Romans formed a hotbed of controversy. The subject of universal argument was "love," and "peace" was a greeting in the market place. In spite of the wisdom and endless debate of men, they could only generally agree that the key to "love" was the key to God, and that to understand one was to understand the other. The interpretations of love ran from one extreme to the other. Some said it was sex, or animal passion relating only to physical gratification; and so developed a philosophy of "free love" which taught that the ultimate expression of devotion to God was fulfilling every lust of the flesh.

Others argued that it was above the physical, and was a "soul to soul" relationship that did not require the physical expression—a love of beauty which embraced all the moral and social graces of the individual. While they preached their philosophy, others believed in only a "performance" kind of love—a mutual relationship that rested solely on the other's ability to provide common pleasure, and included the physical as well as the spiritual.

113

Into this jungle of reason and debate came a man one day, named Jesus. He was God in the flesh, and He came to challenge and destroy every concept of human wisdom. He dwelt among them, and did more than *teach* the essence of real love— He *lived* and demonstrated it. He did not argue with the philosophers; He just loved them, and blew up their world with the undeniable reality of His love. He loved those whom men did not like, ate with sinners and was not defiled, and befriended harlots yet never participated in their lust. He loved His enemies and friends alike, and prayed for those who hated Him. His love crossed every barrier man had erected and broke every rule known to the rulers. It had nothing to do with social strata, race, color, creed, or sex. It embarrassed the Pharisees, stunned the scribes, bewildered the Sadducees, and brought the wrath of all upon Him. Their threats could not stop Him, their plans to destroy Him did not intimidate Him; their persecutions did not discourage nor dismay Him. He just kept on loving, and did to the very end. Religion could not contain His love nor control it. Every boundary they had set soon experienced the velvet steps of His love, and like a rampaging river, it flowed wherever it willed and nothing could stop it.

There were only two reactions to the Love of God in the flesh—men either *hated* Him violently, or *loved* Him passionately. Men either said that He was an imposter, a blasphemer, a devil-possessed madman, or that He was the Son of the living God, Wonderful, Altogether Lovely, the Fairest of ten thousand, and the only Man Who ever revealed the nature of real love. He destroyed the wisdom of the wise by the irresistible nature of His love, for He bestowed love without demanding performance; performed deeds for those who showed no devotion; and loved apart from sex. He was despised, rejected, persecuted, hated, accursed, misunderstood, and finally slain by the wicked hands of those He came to love. At the hour of what they believed to be their triumph over Him and His love, He commended the real nature of His love in dying for the very sins they committed against Him. After three days and nights of relative calm, His enemies were terrified by a worse calamity—the streets of Jerusalem were filled with common, ordinary men and women who were loving with the same power and energy of Jesus' love!!

Like a latent volcano suddenly erupted; like a cascading waterfall, or a river breaking out of its well-defined course, the love of God in those early saints flooded over the land and engulfed it. The unstoppable nature of it swept away every obstacle in its path, and Jesus in them continued to reach out to love the unlovely, embrace the leper, cover the sinner, cross every racial boundary, and engulf the whole world in its flames. The men and women through whom He loved were neither learned nor lettered, but the world took note of them that they had been with Jesus. They had no church building, organization, money in the bank, program, nor public advertisement to draw others to them. They had nothing to sell, offered no musical entertainment, took no collection from the unsaved, and did not glorify their preachers. They just loved . . . loved . . . loved one another with an unearthly, other-worldly kind of love that had first been seen in Jesus. Love was their only distinguishing mark—their only identification. They were not known for their doctrine, creed, denominational name, or achievements—*only their love!* It caused the heathen world to observe, "Behold how these Christians love one another, and how they are ready to die for one another!" A pagan remarked, "They love each other before knowing each other!" and marvelled at a love that never waited on performance or perfection before bestowing itself.

The love that flowed between the early saints of God was like a living *Person,* loving the most defiled, the base, the despised and foolish. Without discrimination that love embraced a black eunuch on his way to Ethiopia; caressed a cruel jailer who had just beaten those who loved him; desired a demon-possessed girl; reached a religious woman leader of a prayer group; melted a mercenary soldier in the Roman army; and made them all one in the mystery of the love of God. The world around them watched in unbelief as Jews embraced the Greeks they had once called "dogs"; males loved females apart from the lust of the flesh; and slaves and masters fell into one another's arms as brothers. That love that destroyed the

116

greatest empire of all history, I say, was like a living *Person,* for indeed it was—*Jesus Christ Himself,* living and loving through the early Christians as He had loved them.

Dear reader, I have taken you on this journey into history only to remind both of us how little we have realized the potential of the love of Christ in us. We are in a similar society where once more "love" is the subject of common debate and the end of all philosophical pursuit. "Peace" is once more a greeting of the street, and those around us are crying out for the "real thing" and putting into music the plea of their hearts: *"What the world needs now is love, sweet love."* The youth of today see the double standards of our love theology and the hypocrisy of religion. Finding no answers in the organized church, they set out on a quest for love that only ends in the same old quagmire of "free love." Disillusioned and desolate, they withdraw deeper into their former hiding places, quit their searching, and sit by silently watching others as they search. Yet we walk among them with the full potential of this same love that changed the course of all history, but we are too busy disputing doctrine; debating social problems; building sanctuaries; entertaining; presenting programs; inventing pious phrases and catchy cliches; vomiting out our religious slogans and claims; but never commending ourselves to them as the learners of Jesus. We wear every kind of religious name, and attempt to designate ourselves as true Christians by the intricacies of

117

our theology; but the hell-bound souls around us watch bewildered as the confusion of this modern Babel grows.

The great artesian well of living water has been capped by the religious world today, and from it they have run their carefully designed lines of plumbing. Each line has its sign, "Baptists only," or "Methodists only," or some other restriction; and from these dripping faucets, those who thirst for love must drink, or not at all. My prayer is that you and I, dear reader, will yield ourselves this moment to Jesus, and beg Him now to love through us whomsoever He longs to love. Let us ask Him now to once more let love flow from God until our own hearts are filled to overflowing, and then spill out of us to others, no matter what the direction.

I am not pleading for a world-wide revival of love. I am appealing to you and me to begin *now,* where we *are,* to let Jesus love one another as He loves us—to accept one another as we are, and to walk in the fellowship of His love with others. If we yield to Him, we shall minister to one another without waiting to be ministered to; serve without waiting to be served; bless and pray for our enemies; recognize one another's faults without condemnation; and labor to perfect each other in love. We shall be sincere, and speak the truth in love to one another; and forbear, forgive and love one another as ourselves. We shall earnestly desire to let Jesus sanctify, cleanse and wash every spot, wrinkle and blemish we see in one another. Let the love of Jesus be the only tie that binds us; and when we cannot approve or understand the other's walk, let us spread over one another the mantle of His love and cover the multitude of our sins. May He seek through us nothing but love, and be satisfied with nothing but love in return. May the Lord Jesus in us show forth His patience, kindness and loving concern. May we learn from Him not to be jealous, boastful, conceited or vulgar. May His love *for* us and *in* us keep us from being irritated with one another, from thinking evil of others or paying any attention when we are wronged. May He teach us to bear one another's burdens in love; believe the best and hope for the best in each other; endure all things; and prove to the world around us that *real* love will never fail. But, what shall I say further about the beauty of His love? As someone said, "The feeling is too big for the word!"

"The love of God is greater far,
  Than tongue or pen can ever tell;
It goes beyond the highest star,
  And reaches to the lowest hell.

"Could we with ink the ocean fill,
  And were the skies of parchment made,
Were every stalk on earth a quill,
  And every man a scribe by trade;
To write the love of God above
  Would drain the ocean dry;

Nor could the scroll contain the whole,
  Tho' stretched from sky to sky."

More important than *telling* it, greater than *writing* it, is to *live* it every day of your life.

THE RELEASE OF LOVE

As you see the smoking flax of love within your breast, you cannot help but wonder if the full potential of love will ever be released. Will the great capacity to love and be loved ever be realized? The answer is a glad and emphatic "Yes!"

"For love is indestructible,
Its holy flame forever burneth;
From heaven it came, to heaven returneth;
Too oft on earth a troubled guest,
At times deceived, at times opprest.
It here is tried and purified
And hath in heaven its perfect rest.
It soweth here with toil and care,
But the harvest time of love is there."

Your eye has never seen, your ear has never heard, and it has never entered into your heart, the things God has prepared for you that love Him and are the called according to His purpose. The depth of His riches in glory for you; the eternal wisdom of the cross; His unsearchable judgments and ways, are past your finding out in this life. Paul was caught up into the third heaven and heard some of these things, but declared that they were unspeakable and not possible to utter while on this earth. Only eternity will fully tell the wonders of His love for you, but enough is written to excite your heart with hope and increase your longing to see the end of God's revelation of Himself to you.

Now, as I prepare to close this book, draw close with your heart while I share with you a glorious secret. It is a mystery made known only to those who have truly received and love our Lord Jesus Christ. Only the heart that knows Him can fully believe and be blessed by this secret I now share with you. *Jesus Himself has promised to come for you!!* Though many saints have fallen asleep (as far as their bodies are concerned) and are now in His presence, He has encouraged us with His promise that some of us *will not* experience death. At an unannounced time, without warning from heaven, the shout of the Lord Jesus will be heard calling you unto Himself. The voice of the archangel and the trump of God will also be heard, and at that moment the bodies of all the sleeping saints will be raised. In a moment, the twinkling of an eye, Jesus will appear in the air above you accompanied by those whose bodies have been raised. He will call you unto Himself as He speaks your name, for this blessed Shepherd knows each of His sheep by name and leads them forth. Face to face with Jesus Christ, you will instantly be fully changed . . . transformed . . . metamorphosed. You will put on fully without what He has made you within, and the preciousness and loveliness that He alone saw in you at Calvary will be manifest for all to behold! Your body is now called a body of humiliation and depression, but then it will no longer depress and humiliate you. Your body, now spoiled and ruined, shall be made incorruptible. Your earthly tabernacle shall be exchanged for an house not made with hands, but eternal. Your vile flesh that has so long shamed and disgraced you and filled you with indignity, shall be glorified. That feeble, weak, diseased body shall be filled with the power of His resurrection life. Your body that was fitted for and controlled by your own depraved nature, shall be fitted for the everlasting control of the Holy Spirit. Your body that was made for earth shall be prepared for and made responsive to heaven. Your body that the grave now seeks to claim in victory shall be made deathless and shall never know death's sting.

Exactly *what* you shall be like has not yet appeared to you, for you shall be made *like Jesus,* and the full revelation of Himself will be in an instant as you see Him *as He is.* Like Lazarus, you will be loosed and let go; the grave clothes of your flesh will fall away, the napkin will be removed from your face, and the likeness of God's dear Son will be unveiled in you. Conformed to His image, beyond the limitations of space — time — matter dimensions, the little man inside will be free forever. All infirmities will be gone; you who have waited upon the Lord will renew your strength, and now the time has come to mount up with the wings of an eagle; to run and not be weary; to walk and not faint. You will hear

123

the voice of your Beloved as He comes saying, *"Rise up, my love, my fair one, and come away. For, lo, the winter is past, the rain is over and gone; The flowers appear . . . the time of the singing is come . . . Arise, my love, my fair one, and come away."*

The daybreak you have longed for will come; the shadows will all flee away; and you will answer with joy that will then be speakable and full of glory, *"My Beloved is mine, and I am His!"*

The Great Shepherd will carry you on His shoulder to His Father's house, where there are many dwelling places, and you will be home at last. The glad hosts of heaven will rejoice with Jesus as He shows that you, His little lamb who once was lost, are now found forever. There you will see the face of Him Who loves you, and time shall be no more. Eternity, composed of ages that will pile themselves upon one another in continuous succession, will begin to unfold the exceeding riches of God's grace, love, and kindness to you in Jesus Christ. You will become His exhibit for all heaven to behold and admire as God's masterpiece of creation. He will read to all the poem of your life into which He poured the essence of His being, LOVE. Jesus will give you to eat of the hidden manna to satisfy your hunger for Himself, and will present you with a white stone in which He has written your name. There, for the first time, you will know fully *who* you are, and *what* He has made you for His glory, and what He *knew* you to be when He said,

*"Thou art precious in my sight . . . I have re-
deemed thee . . . I have loved thee."*

Present with the Lord Who loves you, you will
realize that all the word "home" implies has now
its fulfilment, not in a *place,* but in a wonderful
Person!

The family of God will be there, and friends
you have loved with the love of Jesus shall greet
you. The mighty artesian well of His love will
be uncapped at last, and the full flood of love shall
be released! You will love Jesus as you have always wanted to, and you shall be given the liberty to love the saints with the same fullness of
joy. Unhindered, uninhibited, and uncondemned,
you will love others as He loved you. All the un-
limited potential that man was to have enjoyed
in Eden will be restored; the futility you once
experienced in every earthly endeavor will be
over, and you shall be free to be yourself forever.
Jonathan and David, who kept their love a secret
for fear of the condemnation of others, are now
loosed to walk together in perfect love, and enjoy
each other for eternity. All the desires of your
heart that still remain shall be met and fulfilled.
All the questions that once bothered you are, in
one moment of time, answered forever. *Jesus* is
the answer! *Jesus* is the desire of your heart! Upon
Him, through Him and by Him shall love, sweet
love, flow from your heart.

A victory procession shall make its way
through the golden streets of the New Jerusalem;
past the wall garnished with every kind of pre-

cious stone, with its gates each of a single pearl; past the tree of life laden with eternal fruits for you, to the banks of a pure river of life, clear as crystal, coming from the throne of God and the Lamb. Though the marvels you behold will thrill you—for they are expressions of His love for you, and a part of the unsearchable riches which you shall possess—the most glorious experience of all will be that you are walking with Jesus in white, and He has declared you worthy! As you walk with Him *here* day by day, soon you shall walk with Him *there* to the very throne of God where you will hear the Son of God, Who loved you and gave Himself for *you,* confess your full name before His Father, and before His angels. In Mount Zion, in the midst of the city of the living God, the heavenly Jerusalem; amidst an innumerable company of angels, and the general assembly —the church of the firstborn, whose names are written in heaven; before the face of the God Who is the Judge of all; in the presence of the sprinkled blood; *you*—once a sinner, without strength, ungodly, now made perfect by the perfection of Jesus Christ—shall hear God announce:

"I am not ashamed to be called your God! You are My child in whom I am well pleased. I have begotten you. You are My workmanship in Christ Jesus. I will be to you a Father, and you shall be to Me a child forever. Draw near to me, child, with a true heart in full assurance of faith now made sight, for your heart has been sprinkled from an evil conscience and your body washed with pure water. Let Me wipe every tear from your eyes, for all that made you cry is gone forever."

Now released to express fully the deep thanksgiving and praise that fills your heart, you shall fall down before the Lamb and sing:

"Oh, Lord Jesus, You Who ever loved me and have once and for all loosed me from my sins and self by Your own precious blood, I love You . . . I love You . . . I love You! I, who was once Your enemy in my mind by wicked works; ungodly, without strength, dead in trespasses and sins; ruined, diseased, leprous and spoiled . . . *look at me!* You have made me a king and a priest unto God Your Father forever. Here are the crowns You gave me . . . I cast them at Your feet! Here are the praises You put in my heart . . . I sing them all to Thee. Here is my pitcher filled with the sweet incense of the prayers You prayed through me for Your glory . . . I pour it all out unto Thee. If I had a thousand alabaster boxes, I would break them all at Thy feet. If I possessed a thousand tongues, I would use them all to praise Thee. *Thank you . . . thank you for loving me!"* And He shall answer, "It was my pleasure and my eternal joy."

Around His throne the angels who have listened with bated breath can restrain themselves no longer, and shall shout like the voice of many waters and mighty thunderings:

"Amen! Alleluia! Salvation, and glory, and honour, and power unto the Lord our God. Praise our God! Worthy is the Lamb!! Alleluia For the Lord God omnipotent reigneth."

As you read this chapter, I know your heart does not want to return to earth. As Paul said, it is far better to depart and be with Christ. You are homesick for Jesus as never before, and you know that you are a pilgrim and stranger here, for your home is *with* Him and *in* Him. But listen! *Perhaps today!!* Are you listening? You are not waiting on death, or prophecy to be fulfilled, or events to occur—*you are waiting on Jesus!* In a moment, the twinkling of an eye, you may be in His presence. Before you draw another breath; before your heart beats one more time; before the air now in your lungs leaves you, Jesus may call your name; and you will know more about love than any on earth. Live life moment by moment, for each may be your last, and be comforted by these words of promise. Let the Day Star light the darkness of this moment, and this blessed hope fill you with peace, and purify you as He is pure. Let *"Maranatha"* (our Lord cometh) be your watchword. This secret I have shared with you was revealed to Paul by the Lord Himself. If it were not true, He would have told you. *Our Lord cometh!* Lift up your head; your full release and eternal loosing draws nigh!

"O Lord Jesus, how long, how long
Ere we shout the glad song,
Christ returneth; Hallelujah!
Hallelujah! Amen.
Hallelujah! Amen!"

The End

EPILOGUE

Of the traditions that have come down to us from early Christian writers, one of the most precious is a little story told of John the apostle of love. He was that disciple whom Jesus loved, and the only one of the original twelve who died a natural death. In the eve of his long life he would sit for hours with his learners gathered at his feet. As they listened to him talk and share with them the precious things he had learned from Jesus, one of them said, "John, you always talk about love—God's love for us and our love for one another. Why don't you talk about something else beside love?" John, who as a young man had laid his head on the bosom and heart of God's Love tabernacling in the flesh, answered with joy, "Because there *is* nothing else—just *love . . . love . . . love!*"

"God is love," he had written, and what else is there but God? Love is the true light that came to light every man who was born on earth. Love is the power of life; the energy that holds the universe together; the cause of all creation; the purpose of your existence; and the fullness of God. None of us can preach, teach, talk or write too much about love. The half has never yet been told, and truly there is no cause of stumbling in the man who makes love his only theme.

My five-year-old grandson was overheard one day pretending to preach. With his small New Testament open on the table before him he shouted:

"Jesus loves you! You love Jesus! Nothing to worry about! That's all! Let's sing:

"Jesus loves me! this I know,
  For the Bible tells me so;
Little ones to Him belong;
  They are weak, but He is strong.

"Jesus loves me! loves me still,
  Tho' I'm very weak and ill;
That I might from sin be free,
  Bled and died upon the tree.

"Jesus loves me! He Who died,
  Heaven's gate to open wide;
He will wash away my sin,
  Let His little child come in.

"Jesus loves me! He will stay,
  Close beside me all the way;
Thou hast bled and died for me,
  I will henceforth live for Thee.

"Yes, Jesus loves me!
  Yes, Jesus loves me!
Yes, Jesus loves me!
  My heart now tells me so."

I have taken the liberty to change the last line of that song. I have told you what I know, and declared unto you the record God has given of His Son. I pray that the Holy Spirit has worked in your heart the full persuasion of love and faith, and that you now can say, "Jesus loves *me!* My heart now tells me so." If so, I shall meet you at the feet of Jesus, and He will love us both forever.